The View Over the Wall

Wall

Simon Pollard

To Gillian
Thank you for your patience.
With you
I found
My Peace

CONTENTS

Contents.

1, Introduction 2

Part 1, The Trunk.

2, Energies and Cycles 9

3, Chakras, and Auras. 57

Part 2, We branch Out.

4, The World is Different on water,

or the Choices We Make 68

5, The World Beckons,

Experiencing the Reality, the 5 Senses 77

6, An Unexpected Moment 109

7, the Search for Church (part one) 112

8, Buzzard 122

9, On a Tuesday Night in Sandwich they Play Cricket.............. 127

10, Infrequent Islands of Time (2019) 132

11, Swarm 144

12, The Unexpected Grey Seals 149

13 Osprey 155

14, The Search for Church (part two) 162

15, Unlocking the Web, the 4 Keys 171

Part 3, Look for the Learning.

16, What can We Learn from the Countryside? 204

17, So, What do I Do? 213

18 In Conclusion 224

End Notes 236

The Books I have on My Shelf 238

ACKNOWLEDGMENTS

Gillian, my wife and best friend.
My greatest asset and greatest critic.

Ross, my son and co presenter of the Simple Life Circle.
Wanda, Freya, John and Ash who read the text to make sure it made sense
and enabled me to believe I had a text worth presenting to the world.
Jodie for taking my thoughts and finding images for them.

You all demonstrate the wonder of our place in this world.

And to the

Great Spirit

Balance

Be at Peace

Peace is in balance

Balance is in Nature

Balance in Body

Balance is inside

Balance in Mind

Two magpies bring Balance

As Buzzard flies away

Look to the centre

Of nature.

Chapter One

Introduction

So, it's snowing, and most of the world goes indoors. The roads are treacherous, and the pathways aren't much better. It's cold too, very cold, but the wind's stopped so there's little in the way of a chill factor.

The lights getting low, it's twilight and somehow everything is becoming sharper and more focused. We've already been out and walked the dogs, but Ross, my son, (now an adult) wants to go out and use the sledge he was given four years ago. I am reluctant, the front room is warm, the fire is crackling gently and there is an appealing smell of woodsmoke, the flames are dancing yellow and orange around the timbers I split a few hours ago; but my wife virtually wrestles me into my coat and hat and, laughing I put my boots on and off we go.

Sledging on the drive is not great, there's no gravity to assist us and the snow is very fine and grips too much. We take off for a local slope.

Once there, the first thing I do is fall off and land on my rear so hard it jars my jaw, but do you know what? It doesn't matter. I pick myself up and have another go. Eventually I manage a reasonable slide, not as gracefully as Ross, or over such a long distance.

That matters, and here's why...

You have to live for the moment. If you've read my last book, (the Three Year Pond) and if you haven't, shame on you, you should have, you'll know why this is so important.

So, catch the moment. When people ask me what are the best things about being self-employed, or responsible for my own life and the decisions I make, the first thing I always say is; 'I've been fortunate to never miss a school sports day, or performance, assembly or parents evening through all his time in school.' As a parent these are days that can never be replaced if you miss them, and after that there are so many other events that life presents.

And Ross, at that moment, wanted to go messing about in the snow with his Dad, the first chance we'd had in four years....

In February 2018 Blitz, Scruffy (our dogs) and I got 'driven through,' by a bloke in a pickup truck. We were walking up Church Hill in our village, it was six thirty in the morning, it was dark, but the road is street lit and wide enough for two cars, albeit it would be tight to add a pedestrian and two dogs. We were walking on the right, facing the traffic as you should do, and even though we had seen the driver on many mornings, this morning he just hugged the edge of the road. I'm thinking he'll pull out in a minute, he'll pull out in a minute...' until I realised he wasn't going to. Scruffy was already halfway up the bank. I jumped, but Blitz took the full impact.

I don't think the driver would've stopped if his wing mirror hadn't hit me and flipped back.

Blitz had his pelvis broken in three paces and his femur had been pushed through the socket.

We didn't let him come back round from the sedation he had received for the x rays.

Needless and senseless however you want to look at it. But what it did do was remind me that life is fragile. In one sense and in one way anyway.

....

Have I got your attention?

....

As long ago as I can remember, when my world wasn't working the way I wanted it too or should be, I would take off into the countryside to clear my head and make sense of all those things that were causing me to feel frustration or angst. At least when I was old enough to be out by myself.

I remember becoming a member of the Young Ornithologists Club and when the badge arrived, I sewed it onto an armband and wore it as some kind of military honour. As are many young boys, I was also into guns and warfare and was going to join the army. I read the Warlord comic with boyhood enthusiasm, not realising the reality of the prospect of those dreams.

But despite all those misplaced ideals I innately understood the value of connection to the world we lived. Well maybe not completely innately, we had dogs which needed exercising, we regularly went on picnics in the summer and had days out, often walking and exploring. We would visit many a stately home and explore all the various types of grounds, formal gardens and often associated woodlands. I would charge ahead, eager to see what was around the next corner. Glades of bluebells in the woods in May, or the differing browns and greens as summer faded into autumn.

I don't remember a great deal of learning going on, but a love of outdoors must start somewhere and this had to be as good as any.

Also, it's biophilia*, movement makes us feel alive.

I also had an enduring love for music. All music. As a teenager, when it was all NWOBHM, do you remember that phrase? 'New Wave of British

Heavy Metal'. Iron Maiden, Whitesnake and Saxon amongst others, all of whom still exist. Indeed Maiden and Whitesnake are still headline acts thirty odd years later. I still love the heavy stuff by the way, even the growly shrieky aggressive stuff of today, but I love just about everything else too. I remember my father telling me I would grow out of it and take my pleasure from the more classical orchestral variety, and whilst I do love the latter, I still get a lot of enjoyment from the former.

Whilst at college and through my early twenties I temporarily lost my connection to the outdoors. Well, except as a means of escaping the reproachful eyes of those who liked to think they knew better. Funnily enough, nothings changed.

It was two things I think that brought me back to a more connected view of the world. One was the movie 'The Last of the Mohicans'. It had a profound effect on me. Still one of the greatest movies of all time. A spiritual classic. The whole ethos of the American Indians love and respect for the land and all in it, from the opening scenes where Hawkeye, Chingachcook and Uncas are hunting a deer through the wood; Chingachcook offers a prayer to the animal after it has fallen, a mark of respect, or at the end of the movie when Hawkeye walks into the village of the Mohawks with a sacred belt, telling the history of his people, knowing they would strike him as he did so, and he would face a very likely death for his actions.

But the scene that really struck a chord was when the party of colonials and Indians have taken shelter in the Mohawk burial ground knowing they wouldn't be pursued as a mark of respect for the dead. Hawkeye was explaining to Cora how the Indians viewed the world.

'When the sun and his brother the moon were born, their mother died.

*innate and genetically determined affinity of human beings with the natural world

The sun then gave her body to the earth, and as we know from there springs all life. From her breast the stars were taken and cast into the night sky to remind him of her soul. And from there we should remember all those who have passed'.

Although a fleeting introduction, I think my spiritual journey began there too.

The other point of reconnection would be spending the summer of 1995 in Belarus in Russia doing the practical work of my dissertation. I studied the Non reproductive behaviour of male Montagu Harriers and Marsh Harriers. The latter birds studied whilst staying on a fish farm near Azurney, there were something like 30 nesting pairs of Harriers here as well as a vast array of other birds. We counted over 100 other species.

The Montagus Harriers were nesting in a field forty-five minutes' walk outside Minsk. There were more harriers nesting on this one field than the whole of the UK population. Thus, I started looking at the world around me in greater detail once again.

It was also whilst on a holiday in Scotland a couple of years later that cemented that love of our outdoor world. You cannot help but be in awe of the scenery in Scotland, the lakes and mountains have a majesty that cannot be ignored. We hatched a plan to move North.

The move North never happened, but what it did do was make me look at the countryside on my back doorstep with different eyes and once again I began spending more and more time in the outdoors. That story is contained in 'the Three Year Pond'. The beauty and purity of long-distance walking should be experienced by all. A very pure and simple existence.

I would add here that music and the countryside were the only two long lasting elements of my life, everything else to a certain extent has come and gone. Even the desire to make music, whilst I play a bass guitar fairly well, and have made attempts to play the recorder, clarinet, saxophone and piano, I have never had the singlemindedness to achieve

6

greatness, the same is true of sports. I have tended to have various fads and go into each idea with great enthusiasm and passion, but never with enough determination to see it through...

But love of music and the outdoors have stuck. Meditation struck a chord but didn't get a real hold until I cleared my life of the distractions that we humans celebrate almost as much as life. I stopped smoking in 2015 and this is discussed in 'the Three Year Pond' and finally dispensed with alcohol in 2019. The story of that journey you will find further on.

The real spiritual journey began the year after. I had been asked to join in with an online podcast during the summer of 2020 and as a result of that broadcast I had a meeting with lovely Angela who introduced me to Pranic Healing and the Twin Hearts meditation.

A meditation like I'd never experienced before. Pranic healing is based on understanding of energy and how it is all around us and flowing through us.

Another nudge came from a conversation I had with a family member during 2020. We were talking about what happens after (and before) our time on this world, our physical form. He was rigidly of the opinion that when we die there is nothing. We cease to exist, and everything stops. Our memories, and experiences all just cease unless we have left a written or recorded them. In the same way we are born from nothing, and the 'spark' just ignites. It seemed to me a very fixed view of life and death. There was little room for any other possibility. An absolute view.

That combined with the repeated phraseology of my business coach and mentor Ash that everything in this world was energy. Now the original plan I had for my next book, this book, that I had struggled with, had all the ingredients necessary. That meant I could finally finish the book that I had had in mind since I finished my previous book, the Three Year Pond. It's funny actually, the main body of text in this book (the trunk) was the one section I was really struggling with and had at one point decided to omit. Strangely it is now the main part of the book, the glue that holds everything together. Funny how once again the book I finished writing was a very different book to the one I had intended to write, although at the same time not much has changed.

Briefly, because you've bought the book and I don't want to give it all away now, what you're holding in your hands is a book about our connection to the outside world and the joys of being connected to it. I was also beginning to see that all the indigenous cultures and the religions of the world all had a very similar starting point and contained many of the same elements. I just wasn't sure how to glue them all together. But the discovery of Pranic Healing and then, after a wait of over 30 years before reading 'The autobiography of a Yogi' by Paramhansa Yogananda, a book that had been bought to my attention many years before as a Yes fan who loved 'Tales of Topographic Oceans' gave me all I needed to tackle the main section of the book I had planned 3 years before.

Incidentally, I repeat myself from time to time. It is intentional. I have taken many of them out.

All animals are referred to in the first person, specific. This too, is intentional. Well, unless they are plural!

Energy. And how it pervades everything we do, continually.

The 3 Year Pond was the journey up to the wall, this is a book called...

'The View over the Wall'.

Part 1. The Trunk.

Where it all starts, the stuff that underpins the whole of life on this planet, maybe...

Chapter Two.

Energies and Cycles.

"In physics, energy is the quantitative property that must be transferred to an object in order to perform work on, or to heat, the object.'

That's what we learnt in school, and it's true. Everything is energy, at different levels, whether it's a tree, or how it grows, or the food you prepare and eat, or how you get to work, or the bits that make up the car that takes you to work. Or even you, you are made up of lots of bits and pieces that can be measured and need to have energy transferred to allow you to do anything and usually need some sort of heat transfer to work. Even the winds, clouds pushed by those winds, the seas, and the way they move is affected by those winds and the moon is effectively energy and /or energy transfer.

It all comes down to energy, how it naturally gets used or how we use and transfer it.

In fact, an old college lecturer of mine, a physicist obviously, was of the opinion that everything was physics. Biology was a small part of chemistry and chemistry was a small part of physics, and effectively physics is the study of energy. So ultimately everything is energy and the transfer of energy in one form or another.

The study of energy and how we understand it, is possibly the study of human history or at least, spiritual history. Because, probably unconsciously we have been trying to understand it for most of our time on this earth.

....

Let me explain. If we go back before our established philosophies or religions became the norm, we find a very "connected' way of thinking. A way of thinking or perceiving the world around us, that had us, human beings, as a part of the world rather than isolated from it as many of us are today. It's possible that we are the most disconnected generation, or couple of generations in the history of man. When if you asked anyone, we should be the most connected ever.

Here, in England and associated lands, in Pagan or Celtic spiritual beliefs, due reverence was (is) given to the six realms in ceremony. Earth in the North, Air in the East, Fire in the South and Water in the West. The Gods, Angels, Archangels and Teachers in the Upper Worlds, with our spirit guides, animal guides and ancestors residing in the Lower Worlds. With spirit in the centre binding everything together.

From that starting point everything has a logical home. Associated with earth in the north are all the plants, shrubs and trees that grow from the earth, along with the animals that live within it, as well as all the herbivores that eat the plants growing, cows, antelope, buffalo and snails for example. Taking energy from the sun Earth is the starting point for all life.

That life needs to breathe, so we move to air in the east, giving that life, breath and a voice to communicate with and a medium for that voice to be transmitted; oxygen for animals to breathe and carbon dioxide for plant photosynthesis. And then there are the creatures that live in the air, birds, insects and bats, as well as the viruses and bugs in transit from one organism to another. And don't forget that the air itself moves about as wind. Check out Diagram Three on page 18.

Fire in the south, giving that life passion to live, have imagination to create and make and thus bring balance. With that thought in mind, all the carnivores and predators as well that bring balance to the food chain. Whether that's lions and tigers, or dragonflies living their evolved lifestyles or even us using the power of thought to try and solve problems, real or perceived.

And of course, that life needs to quench it's thirst, so there's water, in the west, to drink, to wash and clean itself and this world in. Few creatures wash the way we do but most need to drink it, either directly or as part of the creatures they eat as prey. Many creatures need water to live in, for part or all of their lives. Water probably holds a greater diversity of life than any other habitat, both in form and also in almost alien lifestyles. It forms 80% of our worlds surface.

The upper world and the lower world, surely, are an attempt to explain that there must be something more than just the physical aspect of life. A metaphysical or spiritual one too. It demonstrates questioning about what happens when we look beyond birth and death. A subject which depending upon your faith, or lack of, is still very much up for discussion today. As my father used to say, 'no one's ever come back to tell us'. It's funny we are so preoccupied with the journey between birth and death, it takes time, tolerance and an open mind to consider there might be another journey that needs some consideration, and that's the journey between death and birth.

This attempt to understand and explain the world also shows an understanding of the natural cycles that determine life if we don't isolate ourselves from them.

....

I have often been heard to ask, 'Were there depressed cavemen?' I think it unlikely, two of the most important facets of life have to be connection to nature, the world we live in, and meaningful human contact. It is likely that once upon a time they may have been central to all thinking, behaviours and fuelled the search for answers.

These concepts seem to have relevance in many other cultures around the world. Cultures that still live and breathe these understandings today.

African tribesmen have a very similar cycle, but they look at life beginning in the east with the fire rising as we move to south which allows us to move, to have motion, do, feel, see and love and hate. To look outward and perform our duties, to live, plan and achieve, to look inward and see the spiritual fire that is our true self. West, the water of our existence, bridging the gap between body and soul, to see family, community and the village.

Native Americans refer to the nations circle in the hoop of the world. In the centre, the bright red stick that becomes the holy tree that gives shelter to the village, in the north where the giant lives, wind and cold giving endurance, the east where the sun, or day break star, always shines giving peace and light, the south, where you always face gives us warmth, and the west, where the thunder beings live giving us rain. Above, the spirit of the sky and below, the spirit of the earth. There is a road between the north and the south, the red road upon which the nation walks, which is crossed by the black road running from the west to the east, the road of troubles and war.

Australian Aboriginies also refer to the dreaming tree of life that connects this world to that of the sky world. The tree has its roots in the air. Shamen climb the tree to receive wonderous messages when the need arises. Souls climb and descend them as is necessary for our physical bodies. This also explains why bodies of the dead are often placed in trees or raised on platforms, so as to help them on their way to the Sky World.

Even the wind whirls in a circle and birds' nests are circles too.

We have the power to plant that tree ourselves and live beneath it, enjoying the shelter and protection it gives, we walk on both roads and use the powers they give, whether thunder, lightning, wind and rain, or sunshine with the benefits of growth learning and peace. The spirit of the air gives us freedom and the spirit of the earth, the wisdom of age.

Our job is to find balance between all these aspects of our natures. For some of us that is personally, for others as leaders.

....

Central to finding our Buddha selves, our Buddha Nature is the belief, the understanding that we are not individuals at all, but a part of a large, interconnected world where everything is connected and sacred. Whether man, small boy, president, animal plant or tree. Human beings are no more important than any other organism on this planet.

People are circles. Without a circle, you cannot have a centre, and there the soul, the divine part of us exists. Cycles once more. Menstrual cycles, where this physical form begins are monthly too, repeating over the same term as lunar cycles. Maybe the female of the species is naturally more connected.

A week is very much a manmade addition, but lunar cycles are obvious, as are seasonal cycles, albeit we possibly seem to be doing our best to remove them from our world, but are based on our tilted equilibrium which also determines our yearly cycle. These cycles clearly show the interconnectedness of everything. See Diagram One.

It's that tilt that makes all the difference, without it life on earth would be very different. If you look at the diagram you will see that the Earth spins on an axis that is tilted. If you imagine a clock surrounding the Earth then our rotational axis is sort of 1 to 7 o' clock rather than 12 to 6. And that makes a huge difference when it comes to our seasons and the length of the day. Our orbit around the sun is elliptical, so you can see the distance between us and the sun changes. We go round the sun once, that is a year. When we are closest to the sun that is the summer,

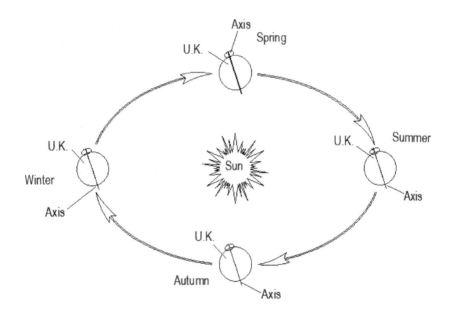

Diagram 1, We move around the sun.

(the left-hand side of our diagram), the top and bottom are spring and autumn accordingly and the right, (when we are furthest from the sun) is the winter. That all makes sense, but it's the tilt of our planet that changes the length of day and night. We (in the UK) are in the top (northern part of the world) and during the winter because of our tilted orbit we see the sun for fewer hours, thus we have shorter days. In the summer our tilt points us towards the sun, we see the sun for longer, therefore our days are longer.

The moon, our little satellite orbits us once every 28 days and with a little observation we can work out pretty much exactly where we are in its rotations because the amount of moon we can see is directly related to its orbital position in relation to the Earth and the sun. See diagram two. The terms new moon and full moon then begin to make sense. Waxing Crescent as we begin to see the moon, then the first quarter. Quarter because the moon is a quarter of the way through it's cycle, waxing gibbous as we see more of the moon and full moon because we can see it all. Our view of the moon then decreases in the same way.

There are 13 lunar cycles per year, so they don't exactly correlate to our Julian year. The week and month are manmade creations to make everything fit numerically. (We currently use the Julian cycle because it fits our current purposes best.) The lunar cycles affect gravity on our earth and keep our orbit stable which we need to be able to live and evolve ourselves.

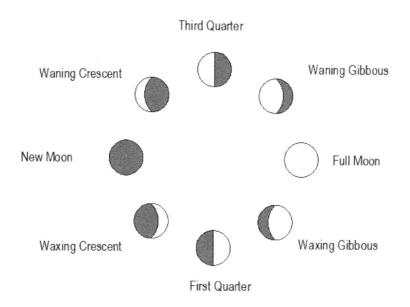

Diagram Two. The Lunar Cycle.

Contrary to common opinion the moon is often not visible at night but can be seen during the day, this is due to its position as stated and how much sunlight it is reflecting, as it emits none of its own.

In Native American culture all these moons have names based on the events that are typical in the natural world, for example, the moon when ponies shed (May) or the moon of falling leaves (November), the months given are obviously approximate.

The symbol of Islam is the crescent moon, and Muslims still operate a 13-month year, which seems to make a lot of sense, certainly more sense than a twelve-month year that we have adopted. They also refer to the Prophet Mohamed as the moon because he 'fully faced the divine sun of truth and was sent to illuminate the dark nights of our soul'. Lovely analogy.

Whilst on the topic of the moon, it makes sense to think about the cycle of a day, obviously day follows night follows day, those of the Muslim faith use the daily cycle as the basis for their call to prayer. There is debate as to whether the day starts just before dawn, or whether it starts the evening before. If the day starts as the sun goes down, a little like the Celtic year starting at Samhain, then the first call to prayer is the evening prayer which symbolises our movement from the light of heaven to the darkness of the Earth, we must die to be reborn. The night prayer comes as darkness turns to night, symbolising actual death. The morning prayer, which occurs just before dawn symbolises the transformation from the forgetfulness of night with the awareness of light. Birth. The noon prayer follows, and this represents the time spent in a physical form, a time of growth, when it's easy to forget who we are and where we came from. The mid-afternoon prayer, which is observed when the sun is descending back to night, life slows down, we reach maturity, and the body weakens and we contemplate or journey back into the forgetfulness of night.

....

There are a lot of symbolic representations and metaphor here. Just consider that as well as the obvious comparison to a human life cycle, there is our relationship to God, and the Earth. Our ego also fits this cycle. Spirituality is all around us.

Even crop planting at these times was determined by lunar cycles, planting is more successful if carried out a couple of days before a new moon, with the harvest carried out on the full moon.

You can see at this point how everything evolves from cycles, for us that begins with the sun and the moon. The Celtic view of life on Earth omits the Sun, but we'll have to forgive them for that. We now know that all energy (that affects us) begins at the sun, without it all life would pretty soon cease. The rest of it makes sense though and science in many ways is proving all this to be correct.

The next step in our life of cycles is the seasons mentioned earlier. There was a time when all life on Earth was dominated by the seasons and the way the weather affected how everything on this planet lived.

The most obvious change is the weather, summers are hot, well warm at the least, winters are cold, rain can become snow and spring and autumn transitionary periods. All creatures on the Earth developed life cycles that mirrored these changes. Nowadays we consider the start of the year as January 1st, an arbitrary choice that fits in with our manmade calendar. Celtic spirituality began the Year at Samhain (Halloween nowadays), a time when the world is quiet and dormant, recharging itself ready to burst forth later in the (next) year. Nature itself seems to proclaim the new Year in what we call spring.

....

Once upon a time humankind also paid homage to these natural cycles in a way that nowadays seems alien to many of us, but deep down is still rooted in our psyche. If you are unsure, just observe your own behaviour when you first go outside. You will take a deep breath of fresh air. Your body remembers... even if you do not.

A good way to look at the cycle of the year is to look further at the Celtic Wheel of the Year. It is firmly rooted in the natural cycles of our Earth and our Solar System and reflects where on the Earth we are and how we evolved to live with that cycle.

Studying diagram three, there are 4 fixed points on the diagram, the longest day, Midsummer usually on the 21st June, the longest night, Yule, like wise in December on the 21st and then the two equinoxes, (when day and night are of equal length) spring and autumn on or about the 21st of March and September. These are the quarter festivals.

Interspersed with them are the cross-quarter festivals, the 'new year 'festival of Samhain in October, Imbalc in February, Beltane in May and Lammas in August. These festivals generally fall on the eve of the

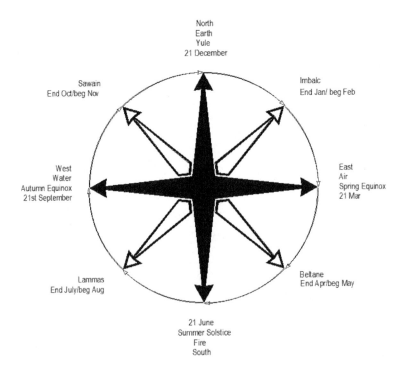

Diagram three. The Celtic Wheel of the Year.

first of the Month. Indeed, we now/still have a bank holiday at Beltane although the purpose of the day has long been lost by many.

So these eight celebrations help to link our lives to the world we are a part of, roughly six weeks apart, they all fall at a time of significant change in our world and if we are watchful of our surroundings make perfect sense. And allow us to recognise when we should be busy and when we should be at rest, and therefore plan for both. A skill that has diminished as we have removed ourselves from the natural cycles of the world we live in.

The wheel of the year begins at Samhain (pronounced sawain), a time of endings and beginnings. The harvest is finished, and the most important task is to prepare for winter; grain is stocked and meat is salted to keep it edible for the cold dark months of the year. Wood is stocked to keep us warm in the winter months. It is also the time when the veil between worlds is at its thinnest and our guides and ancestors can make contact, which is where the modern theme of Halloween and 'ghosts' has probably come from.

The Winter Solstice follows just before our Christmas celebrations, the longest night. For three days and three nights the sun rises and sets in the same place. A time to celebrate the rebirth of the sun and be at peace, sustained by the food we stored and prepared after Samhain. Knowing that we are living life according to the cycles of the world, and that as in all things, where we are is not our final place and that soon the days will get longer, and life will begin anew. Fuelled by our restored and recharged bodies fresh from the winter rest.

At the beginning of February, we celebrate Imbalc. And whilst it's still cold, and days are still short, the first signs of new life and spring are beginning to appear, snowdrops climb out of the earth to find the sun, and signs of the first milk coming from livestock becomes evident, the flowers of hellebores make their appearance and bulbs begin to show green to the world with renewed vigour. It's a time to begin thinking of your plans for the year ahead, whether they are plans anew or picking up where we left off last year. A time to make the ideas we started to think about in the quiet time a planned reality. Readying ourselves for a new year.

Spring Equinox falls in March. The equinoxes are a time of balance, as the day and night are of equal length. We also need to consider own balance, putting ourselves at the top of our agenda. Think of our spiritual, mental, and physical balance as well tuning into our surroundings. This where spring really begins, even our own modern calendar uses the 21st as the first day of spring. Blackthorn is in flower and daffodils are starting to flower, buds are everywhere on trees. The whole world is starting come to life and we should grasp that energy with all our strength. Take those plans that were first thought about at Imbalc and really begin to develop them and reinforce all the relationships around us.

On that note we come to Beltane, everywhere the world is exploding into life, Those creatures that hibernated are awake, the hedgehog and the bat, birdsong is at its highest, waking us up with enthusiasm for the new day, may blossom is painting the countryside white, the woods are blue with bluebells, crops in the fields begin to really reach for the sky. Traditionally people would have built and lit fires, danced around them and maypoles in the first real heat of the sun. A time dare I say, for love and passion and joy in the life to come and the fruition of all we have planned. A time of expectation and celebration for all we have planned. It is likely that before we learned the restraint of Christian and even Victorian piety, there may well have been massed procreation at this time. Interestingly, whilst the thought of pagan behaviours is in mind, I would offer the academic point that originally the word 'pagan' actually meant 'country', a pagan man was a country person! And fertility is obviously a massive transfer of energy.

 Midsummer in June, the longest day. A time to get up early and greet the dawn, followed by a days celebration before watching the sun set. For those tending the world, a time of peace, a time to just be present in the world and rejoice in the gift of life. Banish all doubts and stand strong. The energy in the world is at its greatest, and all our hard work is coming to its fruition and the harvest is soon to come. Revel in all this wonderful world has to offer.

Lammas is the time when the heat of the sun feels most powerful, when all the land begins to look parched, flowers are few and far between and most birds are silent, saving all their energy as they teach newly fledged youngsters how to survive, find food and avoid predators, before the oncoming winter. We begin to reap our harvest in whatever way is appropriate. Traditionally making food and drink from the first samples of our harvest, bread and cake, or even beer and make an offering to the Gods and spirits of our world in thanks for the harvest to come which will sustain us through the year. A time to take pride in our achievements, all that we have worked for within our world...

And finally, the cycle of the year comes to an end at the Autumn Equinox, before beginning again at Sawain. The harvest is in full flight, but as it begins to slow, we cast our minds to preparations for the winter ahead. The countryside is showing a preparedness for regeneration, there's fruit on the hedgerows, full of seed, blackberries are ripe for eating and sloes for mixing with gin. And on that thought, it's another time to be thankful for community and those who we share and support life with. A time to take stock of all we have sown, physically, metaphysically, and communally. The second time of natural balance in the year with day and night once again being of equal length to assess the space around us and what we have done to be a part of all things. To be connected.

These ceremonies also tie in with the elements mentioned before, Earth in the north is part of the celebrations at the winter solstice, air in the east at Ostara, the spring equinox, fire in the south at the summer solstice and water in the west at Lammas. It is then easy to see how they fit, life comes from and returns to the earth, yule, returns to life and grows at Ostara, gains momentum at the summer equinox, before waning at Lammas before returning to the Earth once again at Yule. The cycle then begins again.

21

All life on this Earth is connected in lots of different ways, but before looking at any more examples the concept of Gaia (named after the Greek Goddess who personified the Earth) requires some thought and study. Scientifically, first proposed by James Lovelock in the 1970's, the theory proposes that living organisms interact with each other and their surroundings to form a complex system that maintains and perpetuates life and the conditions required for life on this planet. An unconscious behaviour that helps maintain our world as a healthy vibrant place that allows us all to grow and thrive.

....

So how does all this work? Well, let's keep it as simple as possible and look at a few examples. A first example of a regulatory system is animal and plant. Rabbits eat grasses. You can see this where they have a warren by the side of a field that has some set aside along the edge. The rabbits will eat the grass, and an arc will expand into the field as they eat more and more. The more food that is available, the more rabbits there will be, and as the number of rabbits increases so will the amount they can eat. Rabbit numbers can increase rapidly as they can breed at a rapid rate. Eventually they eat all the food and the number of rabbits that can be sustained with the dwindling food supply will reduced and the weakest rabbits will die. If the available food source doesn't recover, then more rabbits will die. Eventually just a few will survive which will allow the grasses to recover. As the grass recovers so there will be more food for the rabbits to eat.

There are also other factors at work here. As rabbit numbers increase so they will also attract predators, foxes for example, who will react to the increasing availability of an easy meal. As the number of foxes can then increase, so more rabbits will get eaten and the food supply for foxes will diminish. Then the number of foxes will reduce too. With fewer rabbits the grass won't get continually eaten and will recover, until it gets to a level that will support a healthy population of rabbits and the cycle will repeat.

This is a very simplistic version of the cycle, and many other factors will also affect the numbers of both species, a farmer is likely to be one for example, myxomatosis another.

As part of the original explanation for the Gaia hypothesis Lovelock also proposed Daisyworld to demonstrate how plants could also maintain a healthy planetary atmosphere.

Put simply it works like this. There is a planet orbiting a star. The star is slowly getting hotter. The planet is suitable for two species of plant, white daisies and black daisies. White daisies reflect heat and black daisies absorb it.

If you're not sure about this, put on black clothes on a hot day and go out into the sun, then pop back indoors and change into white. You will be cooler for exactly that reason.

At first neither plant does much and growth is slow, but as the stars output increases and the planet starts to heat up so the black daisies have an advantage because they absorb heat and their internal heat rises making them grow and populate faster than white daisies.

As the stars output continues to rise so the black daisies begin to overheat and struggle to maintain growth at the rate they had previously, but the white daisies begin to have an advantage because they can reflect heat and so don't overheat as the black daisies tend to do. As the number of white daisies begins to overtake the number of black daisies the planets ambient temperature cools. Eventually the temperature of the planet gains an equilibrium, regulated by the number of daisies of each colour.

Thus, plants can also regulate the temperature of the planet as well as regulate the gasses that are contained by our ozone layer. A simple example is the balance between animal life and plant life, we breath in various gases, but the important ratio is the one between the oxygen we inhale and the carbon dioxide we exhale due to respiration. Which is balanced by the photosynthesis that plants engage in which takes in that carbon dioxide and releases oxygen. Without that balance neither would survive. As human numbers expand, we should be aware of the need for the forests we are rapidly cutting down...

The natural world is also able to give us examples of its state of health, that are scientifically proven too. Buzzards are a great indicator of a healthy ecosystem, as the 'top' predator, remember the food webs discussed above, they are the first to go when the world below them is unhealthy. Lichens indicate air pollution, if the air is not clean they will die very quickly. Mayfly larvae are only found in very clean water. Clean water is often very clear, but the organisms present are a more reliable way of determining water quality.

As an unqualified observer, the skies have seemed cleaner and views much further this year (2020) without the regular gaseous emissions that have ceased due to worldwide lock down (due to the world pandemic) reducing the use of aeroplanes and juggernauts.

....

There are numerous examples of how many systems within the planet can help regulate the balance. Chapter 15 has various examples of food chains as well, whilst this is all very simplistic it gives an idea of how the planet regulates itself. If you continue with that thought you might say, 'yes, but we are not a part of that cycle anymore', and you might be right, but don't forget we have an inbuilt tendency for self-destruction. Well, maybe not all of us, but a significant number. We have all done things we are ashamed of and most of us keep our errors to a small level. But some of us become major players and manage to start wars or other major disasters; and often cause the so-called environmental disasters inadvertently; these are all ways of keeping the population down, consciously or unconsciously. And it is funny how the disasters we 'cause' seem to gain in scale and regularity as we improve our numbers and our ability to use and abuse technology.

The message is the undeniable fact that the world should be left alone to manage itself, as it had done for millennia, rather than seen as a means of material gain for a misguided ego driven species.

I'm pretty sure there will be evidence of cycles there too.

The pagan though also had an understanding of Gaia, the soil is the skin, rocks the skeleton, the atmosphere the lungs, bodily fluids formed of seas and rivers, oil as blood, nature (all life) makes up the brain and the earths molten core, the heart.

Taking nothing for granted, the pagan would always request permission from the earth or spirit to harvest crops, or take the life of an animal for survival and make recompense by enriching the soil by the use of any available manure, humus or bone meal, making sure that everything was used to its fullest and there was nothing wasted.

....

So, much as we like to think we have a reduced connection to our earth, it's time to actually look at that 'connection', especially as science is beginning to prove an awful lot of the alleged 'hocus pocus' of spirituality may actually have a basis in the science we love so much these days.

As mentioned, central to the teachings of Buddhism is the interconnectedness of everything, having love and respect for the air we breathe and the land we stand on, the animals and plants we eat. And have special reverence for humans because we are the species that has the ability to acknowledge this importance and the cycles that go on within and around us.

There are two simple facts that have a huge effect. We know, absolutely, that all the instructions that go about our body, that tell us we are hot, or cold, or hungry for example, or to go and make a cup of tea, or go to the loo are electrical signals or impulses travelling at great speed to or from our brain to the relevant body part or organ.

They all act at threshold levels, a bit like an anthill. Say, a large number of sensory receptors all realise something we are touching with our hand is too hot they all send signals which go to connectors, a bit like tourists at an airport. When there are enough at one terminal another signal goes on the next journey to the next terminal etc. So, the message goes, until it reaches the brain. The process continues through the brain until a message is sent back to the hand that first sent the message and tells it to move. This all happens so quickly it seems instantaneous. But effectively all these messages are electrical signals.

There's a parallel here too; central to the core of Buddha Nature is the understanding that we are not just a large number of individuals doing our own thing but that all beings and everything are interconnected, just like the signals in our brains.

In fact, we then must consider the fact that if everything on this planet is interdependent then it also has to actually be mutually dependent on everything else. That of course then reminds us that local knowledge is also of great importance. The Tibetan tribesman living in the hills of Kham for example knew exactly where the plants were that they or their animals were that would sustain them, and how the weather and seasons would change due to their cycles, as did the Australian Aboriginies in the deserts of their homelands.

It is only now that we buy most of our foods from supermarkets and live in well-built and well insulated houses that these cycles have escaped us. Also losing respect for life and death, how many of us would eat meat these days if we had to do the butchering of the animals we had nurtured since birth? It is an understanding of natural cycles and the way our earth works that allows all these processes to continue with respect.

And that then begs the question, how much compassion do we show to the world we live in, the world that nourishes us, the world we live in? Often we are lost in a pursuit of self interest…

Now we also know that at the core of our earth there is a massive burning furnace and electromagnetic fields, and all through the solar system these are prevalent. And electricity is affected by these fields. This can be demonstrated in a laboratory or even in electrical kits we buy our children.

Another example is based on the fact that we are 70% water, we know how the moon can affect the oceans, with high and low tides and the extremes of spring or neap tides. In fact, this is where the phrase lunatic comes from. Indeed, fiction writers have gone even further and used the moon as the trigger for werewolves.

Which might explain, at least in part, why we can't explain why we feel the way we do on occasions, which often during a full moon. If only we were aware of it.

There can be no doubt of our interconnectedness with the natural world. Whether because there was a need to understand it for our survival, or spiritually, for connection, or because as a part of the living breathing massive super organism, we needed to receive the necessary information to look after our world. Surely, we have a responsibility as caretakers. And that was the responsibility of the Green man who was once given due reverence and his example was followed. Certainly, we did a better job in days of old, before decisions could only be taken if justified by science.

Also, it might suggest that there is a real basis for the claims of astrology.

....

Now that then leads us to the subject that has been the source of philosophical discussion for eons. The soul, that 'thing' that binds us together and makes us more than the sum of our parts. We need to think a little more about what exactly it is, or might be. As an organism, as is everything that grows upon this planet is, whether animal, plant or microbe, is made up of measurable things that have a purpose within us, at whatever scale we choose to use, cells, organs, or body parts and can be measured and studied. Cells make up organs or bones and organs and bones make up limbs which are surrounded by our largest organ our skin. Plants are largely the same, as are all the things on this planet. But to make all this work we need some kind of glue. Something that gives any organism the drive to do anything, to actually live, to reproduce and eventually die, at which point it leaves us. Our soul. The question of whether the soul is part of us, or separate is discussed later, an awesome dilemma for thought on its own.

But here is the important bit, all of those parts mentioned above can be separated and studied in isolation and then put back together, but then the "soul' or spark, or whatever it is, is not there, the important bit is missing. If this seems a bit peculiar, think of it another way. A room has a magic or a life to it, in the way that we make a house a home, it the space inside that gives a room 'life'. If you take the four walls, the floor and the ceiling and lay them on the floor, all the parts are there, but the magic is gone. What's important is hard to define but is determined by what you can't see. The total is more than the sum of the parts.

Another interesting concept to think about, is whether the words and concepts of soul and energy can be interchanged, are they the same, or slightly different versions of the same thing.

But if we accept the soul is the life force that stays with us whilst we enjoy our brief physical time on this Earth that then suggests it must be somewhere before we get 'it' and goes somewhere after we cease to need 'it'. We mentioned this above. And there's a cycle there too.

If we return to the fact that everything is energy, we then need to remember that Einstein in his first law of thermodynamics stated that energy can neither be created nor destroyed, which as far as we can tell is true by every test we have been able to construct to challenge it, we have to consider the idea that a soul cannot either be created or destroyed either.

That is a big concept to get our heads around. Especially as we cannot measure a soul. Yet. That's a challenge for meta physicists to undertake. But lends some explanation to the idea of ghosts or other unexplained phenomena; maybe.

....

Maybe the answers are in the many and varied belief systems that permeate the whole of our world. Whilst religion or belief systems are many and varied, they seek to offer their disciples answers to the mysteries of life that many of us (myself included, probably, for now) don't know and feel we cannot know. After all birth and death, and a need to celebrate and revere these parts of our lifecycle are surely one of the most important facets that make us human.

The Tau te Ching and Hindu Scripture both suggest that this life-giving force is eternal and this physical part of it is temporary and fleeting. The Tou te Ching is the collections of essays left by Lou Tzu, a wise Chinese sage who lived 2,500 years ago. His writings were in a language possibly vague at best and have been interpreted many times over the years or centuries. But in essence they are life or mind opening or altering. In Hindu Scripture at death our soul returns to 'God' for a fleeting re union, having achieved whatever purpose required us to be on this Earth. Studies of any Hindu Yogi are full of examples, many of whom even ready their closest disciples for their imminent and foreseen departures.

In Buddhism a, a Tulku is a reincarnate Lama (high priest). Reincarnation is driven by Karma, the purpose of this life is to purify our thoughts words and actions until we attain Nirvana. The success we have in this life can affect the next life we have. A lama who achieves Nirvana will choose to return to continue his compassionate work. There is a story of the sixteenth Karmapa (head of a branch of Tibetan Buddhism) collecting caged birds whilst touring America. They were his previous disciples that he was returning to freedom.

When a religious leader is dying, he will make preparations for his forthcoming death and leave instructions with close disciples, often leaving clues for written instructions that can only be found after his death with instructions as to where he will be found in his new 'life'. Who his parents will be and how to ensure it is him reincarnated. A labrang (building) is set up to look after the belongings a deceased Lama leaves, ready for his use in his next 'life'. The next life maybe into different class of society too, working class or wealthy is not a condition for reincarnation.

Lama Yeshe Losal Rinpoche, tells the story of how his brother Tulku Akong Rinpoche had asked the Sixteenth Karmapa if he could have one of his teeth as a keepsake after his body had been cremated. Akong could not be there at his cremation so did not get the tooth.

Eleven years later when his reincarnated body was found, Akong asked the boy if he had anything for him, he collected a milk tooth he had kept especially. The child became the seventeenth Karmapa and had the abilities and attitudes of the adult Sixteenth Karmapa.

African Shamen also teach that when someone dies on one world, there is grief, whilst on another there is joy, inferring that the souls simple moves on from one physical body realm to another. The Tou te Ching is full of examples of this thinking too.

Australian Aboriginies believe that when we die we return to the 'dreamtime', the source of creation, where all life springs from and returns to. A spirit can sometimes linger on the way and this is where a ghost or essence has a time of existence. When there, the soul or djang waits to be reborn.

Muslims believe that the journey to heaven is not something you earn during life, but something you can learn to receive during life. Lovely distinction.

American Indians will tell you we go from childhood to childhood. An often easy, albeit unsettling analogy. When a medicine man is preparing for a healing ceremony, he will dance beginning in the north, moving to the east, 'where' life begins, passing to the south, the source of all life at its most energetic, where the 'flowering stick' comes from, before moving to the west, the setting sun of life before we move back to the north, where we the 'white hairs' are, he gives his life back to 'all life'. If he then lives, he returns to the east and childhood. Wonderful belief system. Naturally, all actual healing is done facing south...

African Shamen also teach that we come from other 'planets' to perform a task here and that is to help, or receive help as required. The initiation as they leave childhood and become an adult is for serious people to go and see what their purpose is, whilst those who are not serious about their purpose will not return. Again, the physical body remains whilst the soul makes the journey. The impression I have reading the recitations is similar to that of the analogy between an anthill and the operation of a brain and the electric signals, our souls are the electric signals of a greater intelligence functioning on a far greater scale. And that leads to great questions of fate and freewill. The analogy goes even further, a community is a living breathing organism, and all the people are merely cells that make up that organism. All bad cells are removed at initiations... Gaia in evidence again.

Other journeys involve going back before our birth and finding out our purpose on the earth and similarities with Hindu perceptions occur. I love the concept of journeying from death to birth. Any change in our belief in the journey from birth to death is intoxicating... Often we live our lives between the death on this world to birth on another and so we live that life until it comes to an end and we either return to this world or go to another.

....

If our soul is energy, and what else can it be, and as we know that energy can neither be created nor destroyed, then surely it cannot cease to exist. What is certain though, that whether we believe in reincarnation or not, the loss of anyone we are close to will always be just as hard hitting. We still have to deal with the emotions that go with it.

The African Shamen also teach that 'some people live in order to remember and some live because they do remember'. That is a real mind bender, which are you? I know that when I 'find' something that is right, the pursuit of it is, within reason, easy, fairly simply accomplished, almost as if it is prescribed. A greater plan? Maybe, but other things are so difficult. I know there's always a question of freewill, but for me, doing the 'right thing', feels good. It is almost as if I am fulfilling my purpose. Mind you, sometimes, it is right to battle through to a goal if it feels 'right'. Its purpose, pre-ordained, and innate, or something that comes out of the way we are 'made', evolved, or something we have become as a result of our personal past. Having said that, the idea of fate, which infers we have no freewill is just as disturbing?

For the Native Americans, the visions themselves give meanings and a purpose, Black Elk, a Sioux medicine man speaks of the vision he had aged nine that revealed his purpose as a medicine man of his tribe and the people.

A vision once received must then be given to the people so that they know its intent and its content. Often during a vision dance the sick are healed and the people's purpose and future goodwill is delivered resulting in happiness and exultation. The connection to the spirits and their world is made. The message also must be told to the people through dance and ceremony, the holy man has a duty to impart this information to gain release and peace for himself. It can be difficult to separate where the spirit (real) world and the world we inhabit begins and ends.

A ceremony would include all tribal members and many of the animals, usually horses and involve a lot of singing, chanting and dancing, praising the gods as well as celebrating the message.

Taking one step aside the sense of community that these ceremonies must have invoked must have been huge and further install the sense of belonging. Which after all as humans of any culture we all seek, one way or another. As we said before, connection and meaningful human contact.

Indeed, Black Elk goes further, it is through visions that a man gains his power. Crazy horse had a vision, he visited the spirit world, the 'real' world. Everything there was a spirit, there was nothing hard or real. He saw a horse that was a shadow that danced in a crazy way. It is from this vision that he got his power. Whenever he thought about his power, he became invincible. He was undefeated in battle. His capture by the 'whites' was by treachery, they removed him from the circle, he then lost his power and then they killed him. So much to infer from that story….

The Australian Aboriginies have sacred spaces where the energy (djang) of their ancestors goes and can be recalled when needed during ceremony.

Ceremony, dance, singing and chanting, as well as the obvious meanings for community, and a desire to generate a desired outcome may also have greater significance if the frequencies have a resonance with the earth itself. Resonant frequencies are frequencies that magnify if they match the surroundings. This can be beneficial and undesirable. All things have a resonant frequency. You may have noticed how if the engine of your car is at a certain rpm the rest of the car seems to vibrate much more, this is because the resonant frequency of the car body is the same as the engine. Just imagine if a large group of people were singing and dancing at the same frequency as that of the earth, or even our brainwaves what the result might be. All of a sudden, the need for ceremony becomes clear on another level, connection to the earth. Either way messages are coming from and being sent to the earth, as well as the community. Mind bogglingly awesome.

It is said that the power of seven people meditating together is the same as one hundred meditating separately. Think of all that energy being channeled at once, the power of connection.

....

The soil of our Earth can be used to transmit signals and thus messages too. The process stopped when the amount of signals being sent caused confusion and the need for secrecy arose. Put simply if two electrodes are inserted into the ground and signals such as morse code are used the signal will transmit without the need for any other connection for a mile or more and be received the same way. Very similar to the rhythmic nature of ceremony, with lots of singing and dancing. A physical connection to our world becomes very feasible, even imaginable to our modern sensibilities.

Often for the Aboriginies, messages are given during the 'dreaming'. A place between sleep and waking, I think we have all been there on occasion, and it's sometimes amazing how 'right' some of the things we see there are. If we remember these messages, (it's important to write them down) before we forget them, as we always seem to do, then when we look back, we are pleased we followed through with these messages. I am sure you can half remember one or two.

When Muslims give praise they assume a position of prostration, they lower themselves to their knees and then lower their head to the ground with their arms outstretched. This puts the heart above the head. The heart gains dominion over the busy clutter of our brains, which then benefit from increased blood flow, and it is also possible this helps relieve stress and depression. We also become grounded, literally as well as metaphorically. Physically we release or discharge electrostatic charges from our bodies, and we have plenty enough of those, which we transfer for healing electrons. Which helps restore the balance we need to function fully. Obviously, it helps to feel humble to the majesty of the world around us too.

....

If you think back to the Gaia concept of the Earth, then the idea that we are the 'ants' running around the earth functioning unconsciously as the signals of a super brain, it is possible to make a comparison with these similar ideas and concepts.

 What is clear though is that there are many hints, tips and suggestions given to us from the world around us, it is still up to us to interpret that information into a path that helps ourselves and those around us. We should look for the learning in everything in our world, constantly.

A man's power comes from understanding, understanding visions, understanding ceremony, understanding people and understanding the world we live in.

There are places where the 'veil' between worlds is thinner and all journeys are taken there, these places are often far from the community, hence another need to enact the vision upon returning. The message clearer through the act of a dramatic event rather than straight story telling. I definitely understand and empathise with this 'theory', there are definitely places that have a 'specialness' to them. Sometimes because of where they are, or what they are and sometimes because of what we make them.

....

There's a cabin we started using purely as somewhere to get away from work, social media and the phone. Whilst not far from the beaten track, it is fairly isolated and the view from all windows is green. There are tall ash trees and sycamores, as well as hawthorns. There are shrubs, hydrangeas, roses and salvias, hedgerows of privet and cotoneaster. The cabin itself is nothing exceptional. Wooden in construction, with a bedroom, bathroom and a kitchen diner living room. All facilities are basic, the shower is erratic, there's no bath, or plug for the basin. The easy chairs are not very comfortable, but none of this matters. It's an oasis, a place out of time where very little changes. We keep going back because there's just a little magic there. We are always sad to leave. It's amazing the great things that have begun or evolved from there. The future change of focus for the business I run came out of planning sessions held there. This book has been on the writing process almost since 'the three year pond' was unleashed onto the world, but it was at this cabin that I finally found the inspiration, motivation, or the direction that fed these needs, and the book is now well underway (you're reading it)! There's just a magic there that enables us to find solutions or solve problems that we don't manage anywhere else. Real or perceived? Don't know, but there's something there.

After a stay there's always an excitement to put whatever has been planned into motion. Back to the real world.

And at home, the area under the copper beech tree. Now the most amazingly peaceful and calming place ever. The space has always been there (obviously), but the addition of water has transformed it totally. Initially a massive compost heap when I first came to be here. It went through various transformations before it became a decked area, another place to sit and have a cuppa in the garden. But still it was unused and became a dumping ground. Possibly because it never really saw any sun. So, move on a couple of years and my wife has made the house and garden 'our' home and we decided the time was right to make the area our pond.

The copper beech tree is probably about seventy years old. I vaguely remember talking to the elderly lady who lived in the cottage behind us when I moved in, and she told me she thought her husband had planted it in about 1950. They had lived in our house before building the bungalow behind us and subsequently moving in.

The tree is huge, probably forty or fifty metres high and has a diameter of similar proportions, it regains its leaves fairly late in spring, but they are the most magnificent in their 'coppery' ness. You can pick the tree out from a long distance out into the countryside because of its colour. Grass had always been difficult to grow because of the amount of water the tree took from the ground, so it was surrounded by flower beds, pathways and decking.

We had always planned to install a pond, and this was the perfect place. The decking was removed, and the area dug out. The pond would be on two levels, an upper one kept largely clear for paddling and meditation, with water emerging here, pumped up from the lower pond and then cascading back into a wildlife pond, the planting, such as grasses, loosestrife, caltha and elodea and an emerging soil substrate providing the habitat for numerous invertebrates and amphibians that would hopefully decide to live there.

The decking was reconstructed over part of the upper pond allowing two people to sit comfortably or grandchildren to catch plastic ducks.

An amazing place to sit, find peace and meditate. The heat of the sun warming you until the canopy grows and dapple out the sun as woodlands do, but then provides welcome shade from the intensity of the summer sun in July and August.

What we had not expected, as the planting matured, was the 'energy' that was available in this spot. Just being there gave a sense of being alive in a way that few other places do. Whether enhanced by the water, or the sound of water it's hard to tell, but all who come and spend time there struggle to leave the sense of peace and calm and general wellbeing that is found in this spot. We use it all the time. I can often be found in meditation there early on most mornings. I believe the inclusion of water in this place has increased the energy substantially, allowing greater connection to this world.

....

The word 'grove' means a clearing or sacred space in the woods, a place cleared to enable a gathering of people to celebrate, give due reverence and to connect with the natural spirit, real or perceived. Places of power. There is no doubt that surrounded by trees there is feeling of life and healing and wellbeing that is thankfully becoming more and more felt and understood in these days of disconnection and science. Trees have a heartbeat, but it's barely perceptible, maybe it's just so slow it's not obvious to our busy minds unless we slow our thinking down to a similar level of understanding. Trees certainly have to pump all that sap up the trunk out into the branches and then the twigs and finally the leaves and order to survive and grow. It is also worth noting that trees are the most efficient liquid pumps on this planet. With all the technology we have at our disposal we do not have anything as efficient as a tree. We can learn a lot, I think, from trees.

I read recently how trees might actually communicate with each other using the vast fungal network that stretches far and wide in the soil of our world. The wood wide web. Maybe the 'Tree of Souls' in Avatar is not so far-fetched after all.

The subject of Ley Lines then must also be considered. These groves and other sacred places, stone circles, henges, wells etc, and commonly now, churches, are often 'on lines' that cross the world. If you look at a map and use a ruler it is surprising how often this is the case. Check out the churches of Cheavening, Seal, Seal Chart, Ightham, Barming and Bearstead. And there are several others very close to the line. Whatever the correct explanation, and there must be one, you have to wonder are we now missing something here.

Possibly the two greatest or most well-known sacred places would be the Black Hills of South Dakota and Uluru (Ayers Rock) in Australia.

....

Returning to the subject of meditation, the link between visions and dreams and journeying becomes blurred, the only constant is our consciousness, and then probably our sub conscious. If you spend enough time in silence out in the countryside and listen, you can hear the worlds beating heart. Everything on this earth has a beating heart, all animals, birds, insects and other creatures, and as we mentioned trees too. If you are still for long enough and listen hard enough it becomes perceptible.

Australian Aboriginies believe in this 'interconnectedness' at the very heart of their philosophy or spirituality. Everything began in the 'dreamtime', all life whether plant or animal, physical or spiritual. Even rocks and minerals.

It's funny how the two philosophies of indigenous cultures and our modern world are poles apart and that all attempts to bring them together has usually come from the indigenous rather than from us. Maybe it's due to a differing degree of tolerance, as well as an attitude that teaches acceptance rather than greed. The Aboriginies had the concept of kinship at the heart of their traditions, every arrival or settler could be absorbed into the tribal unity if their behaviour was kindly.

I recently read of a wonderful experiment where people of Asia and the far east and the Americas were shown a picture of a man addressing a crowd and asked to describe it. The westerners (Americans), almost all described the man first and the crowd as an afterthought; those from the east described the crowd first. They also then described the little girl on her own from a crowd of children. Those children from the west, that she is happy, because separation is OK for us and those from the east, that she is sad because she is separated. It's funny I guess how one culture tries to keep hold of its traditions whilst the other has a history of trying to remove it from the other.

The benefits and hazards of the properties of one tree or plant become understandable and decipherable, and how those relationships change from one organism to another. The whole of nature almost becomes one 'consciousness'. Gaia again.

Buddhism and Hinduism, both religions and philosophies from the 'old, eastern' part of the world focus very much on looking inwards, into their own natures to find mental and spiritual peace, while we of a western mind tend to look outwards. Central to these religions, Buddha nature, as mentioned earlier, suggests that rather than looking to material possessions, attaining social position or wealth to achieve happiness, as many do, we should begin to realise that happiness comes from within.

In the Muslim teachings it is suggested you already have everything you will ever need during life, it's just a matter of learning how to tap into our unknown potential. "God is everywhere in everything all around us all the time."

Have gratitude for the wonderful things we already have around us, accept all gifts, even those we do not want and enjoy them for what they are, those unexpected visitors who arrive just when you are about to sit down to listen to the CD you just bought or a book you have been wanting to read as your reward for the days hard work. Let them in and enjoy their company with good grace. Begin to realise that the only thing that matters is right now. What happened yesterday is gone and tomorrow is not here yet. What is happening right now is a gift called the present. Where you are? Who you are with? What you are doing?

There was a telly programme when I was a teenager called Kung Fu. The central character, Grasshopper, I think, in one episode had been wrongly convicted of murder and was travelling to his place of execution. He sat calmly in the trailer he was in. Another convicted murderer who was guilty was beside himself with anxiety and distress, even though he knew he was guilty, and his punishment was just, asked Grasshopper, why he could sit there so calmly. Grasshopper replied, 'If I worry will the future change?' I have never forgotten this sage piece of advice, but often struggled to implement it; but it is so true.

....

Another step is to think about the oneness of everything, the more we know the less the need to give everything a name. It's just us in our western culture that needs to name everything and sort it and classify it, but nothing out there knows it has a name and could not care less about it. A tree just 'is'. A fox just is, it just does what it does, it has no need or requirement to know it is a fox, it has no need to know that it has caught and is devouring a rabbit. It surely follows that the more we perceive that we know, the more we should let go and just seek connection, the greater the connection, the more the understanding

40

and the less need there is to know.

It is then a small step to gain some control over the inner chatter that we bombard ourselves with continually. Disconnect from our inner dialogue of often uncontrolled thoughts and listen to the unbiased messages that come from the world around us when we find the peace and stillness that connection with mother nature provides and engage with that. Acknowledge all thoughts, but let the unhelpful ones go.

Just think, have you ever managed to be totally engaged in what you are doing at that moment and not consumed by yesterday, or tomorrow, or the good wishes and intentions of others. It's not easy to exist in the present moment, and that moment alone. But it's worth practising.

Buddha had a brilliant story about the obstacles and difficulties we have to experience and deal with in life. He related these to arrows, we all get struck by the first, the actual hurt itself; when we lose someone close to us, or a job. Get into conflict with those around us, at home, at work or even socially, or when people don't behave as we would like them too. The second is the way we react to this hurt. This arrow arrives in the same place as the first and really drives home the hurt and the loss. Often then we attempt to hide or numb the pain, with drugs, alcohol or sex, we can become controlling or very busy at work or a project. The hurt doesn't go away, we just get a short term 'fix'.

The third arrow is the one that does the real damage, we decide that the problem is not the actual issue itself, but something to do with us personally, we are flawed and deserve what has happened. I think we have all been there at some point or another. But we must learn to disconnect these events from ourselves. Ultimately all these things are obstacles that we have to learn to use as opportunities for growth. They are our lives.

Compassion then, is needed, everywhere. For ourselves first. We are all valuable people. And then for everybody else. Even those who intentionally, or unintentionally arouse negative thought or feelings or want to cause us harm. Compassion and forgiveness are the key to happiness surely. There is another lovely analogy from Buddhism to consider. The symbol of compassion is the lotus flower. The flower blooms atop a beautiful lake and is stunningly beautiful. But the roots grow in the dirty stinking mud at the bottom of the lake. It is here that all our trouble and obstacles reside, all those things we have to deal with and struggle with, but give us all the opportunity to deal with, in actuality and also internally, that allow us to bloom and become the beautiful people we are all capable of becoming. Another example is that of the hoverfly, pretty little insect that lays its eggs in stagnant pools.

....

At the heart of all that growth has to be our soul, that unknown, unseen component that resides in all of us, and has done so since time began and will do so for ever.

This is difficult for us to accept in our western cultures as we are so deeply entrenched in our belief that if we can't test it by scientific methods then it cannot be true! But if we believe in a soul which we can't measure, then surely, we have to be open minded. For myself, my Grandmother knew she was nearing the end of her time on this earth, she was arranging all her affairs with a precision and more definition than you would put into a will. She also knew that her last important task on this earth was to attend my first wedding. Having assured herself that all was well with those she loved she passed away. (She had a stroke whilst we were on honeymoon and died a couple of days after we returned). She had completed what she needed to do.

It was the same with my mother and my father-in-law (see the Three Year Pond). I knew myself when I left my father-in-law that day, that that would be the last time I saw him alive. What is important here is that they were ready to go, even if their life had been cut short by illness, as was the case with my father in law, he had plenty of warning, and not by sudden illness or accident. Hindu beliefs state that an experienced Yogi can also cure serious illness, this is another belief difficult for us in the West.

In the late eighteenth century as the 'old ways' were coming to an end for the North American Indian. As we, the white man with all our greed and desire for more than we can ever use, stole all of America away from those who had cared for the land for longer than mankind has memory, a saviour arose, who they likened to our Jesus. A man who was in touch, connected, with our world as well as the world of gods and ancestors, as Jesus was. Someone who could connect us with the real meaning of the world. His ultimate fate was easy to predict.

  The point being that if we, possibly spiritually innocent, folk in our western Cultures have even an inkling of an idea of the nature of life and death, those from a very much more spiritual and/or indigenous culture can teach us a great deal, but the nature of life and death being a cycle and the soul being eternal is quite possibly not so far from the truth.

....

Now whether attached to us or not, our soul must be centred somewhere and it is likely that as it's the centre of everything we as organisms, with conscious minds do, the soul at least functions through our brains and that presents another interesting dilemma. It is likely that our brain has a small percentage of conscious thought with the rest being unconscious. The ratio is greatly in favour of much of what we think of as being unconscious thought, and probably rightly so, put it this way, if you had to actually remember to do everything you needed to do your brain couldn't cope. Let us think about it in basic bodily functions, you had to remember to breathe or make your heart pump, you'd definitely die if you went to sleep, and whilst many of the things that happen in your body are chemical reactions, many of them have to be 'controlled' in some way. That is done by the subconscious part of your brain. Which also does a lot of the thinking you need to do, which is why some times ideas just 'pop' into your mind, your sub conscious has been beavering away on your behalf with the information its gleaned from your conscious. That gives even more meaning to the phrase, be careful what you wish for because you just might get it. Be careful what you think about too. The law of attraction was discussed in some depth in 'The Three Year Pond'. There is no doubt, having more experience of working with it now than before, when you are conscious of what you are thinking, what you are doing and where you are going, you are far more successful and happier than when you lose track of your desires and your direction.

I mentioned earlier that we are only using a small percentage of our brain to do all these activities and that still begs the question, 'what's the rest of it for?'

Whilst stories of aliens coming back to give us the next 'instalment' of development are appealing, it's probably unlikely, after all look at our own history. Every time a culture discovers a more 'primitive', culture (I use the word carefully), we have a tendency to try to destroy or at least utilise it for our own ends. Look at the discovery of African Tribesmen, Australian Aboriginals or American Indians as easy examples from our own history. Sometimes it is difficult to be British and proud. If any alien species had found its way here, it would have technology far in excess of ours and we would have to be careful of its motives in case it's like many of us.

It also absolves us of a certain amount of responsibility and that is never a good thing.

....

But this of course could just be the inherent 'fear' that is inbred into the society we live in. So many of us are living in partial or complete fear. 'No I'm not!', you might say at this point. Are you afraid of losing your job? Or your house? Or a loved one? Or getting cancer? Of what you said last night when you were drunk, or what you might have said when drunk but can't remember? Or what the next bank balance will say? Or the fact that no matter how much you try you just can't live within your means? Or that the fact that our society continually tells us we don't have enough? And that we need the next new phone, TV, car, house, gadget or X box. Or whether you have enough wine for the next social event. The list is endless.

Do you have the strength or wherewithal to remove all these pressures from your life?

....

It is far more likely that we knew something we have long since lost. There is growing talk these days of a super consciousness, an ability to connect with a higher source of reality or having a greater understanding of spirituality and the life-giving force that sustains us and envelops us if we just choose to embrace it and adopt it as a life practice. Soul? Gaia, God? Call it what you will.

And then there's more than one theory as to how this whole soul, life, 'God' even, is structured for want of a better world. Is there a vast collection of souls existing in a metaphysical sense, kind of in parallel as we do in a more physical sense? Or is this all-enveloping source of life more like a large enveloping blanket that we are all drawn from, almost like from a large pipette. And if that's the case then there are lots of other interesting questions as to what might be going on.

Are we unconsciously part of a very large hive mind? Whilst we have the choice to do exactly what we choose; we also seem to have a pre-ordained purpose too. Free will and divine will if you like. That would fit with the concept suggested above. Or are we more separate than that? More like a jigsaw puzzle. Whilst a part of the larger whole thing, but all separate and distinct. It is likely then that the end result is the same as far as freewill is concerned, but do we then leave a 'hole' that we were previously filling when we return to earth and a new body?

And as I said before, 'what about fate?'

It then follows that this super being, thing, God, whatever we choose to call it must have some kind of geographical element to it, if we are all to understand how to live in a certain location. No use dropping a Plains Indian in the arctic and expecting him to know how to live. Of course, that then begs the question, how much thought is innate, or known, but needs tapping into, if we only knew how. And is that the sub conscious thoughts that pop into our head unexpectedly. And of course, some is taught due to tradition!

....

An example of what is known innately can be understood by considering the migration behaviour of a swallow. The adults spend the summer here, (in England and the North) and raise their young, before departing in August to return to South Africa to over winter. They don't take their young with them. The swallows you see flying around in September are the pristinely feather youngsters. The bedraggled adults have gone.

The young, newly fledged juveniles find their way south without any guide at all. Whether they know the way, or know the way markers, or know how to read the light on the horizon, or whatever is a mystery. But know it they do and it is not a behaviour taught to them by the adults. They just know it. Innately!

Would that explain why we only 'maybe' use a small part of our brains, if that is the case, because the other part holds information from past lives.... Or is it so that the aliens can come back and top us up when we're ready. And how, incidentally will they know when we're ready.

It is surely more fulfilling (simpler?) to believe in a souls return though and strive to further the good work a person has done so that if they do return they can see the value of their past life. It also gives more purpose to the lives we are currently enjoying. Karma!

....

Reading any text, so far, on any religion, of any culture anywhere in the world refers to an 'other' world or reality, or both. The Celtic 'upper' world and lower world mentioned above, the African 'altered' reality, where not all travellers return from, a world where the living beings appear in divine spirit form, the Yila tree, a green spirit lady for example, there is spirit in anything, everything. It is in how you look that determines what you see.

It might be the right time then to look at the fairy tales we have in our culture and the folk that live in them and wonder about them. Are they stories that are trying to teach us about the connections we have lost? Elves living in and caring for the trees of the world, dwarves in caves beneath the world, fairies, pixies and goblins in other worlds. They are none of them that far from the stories of other worlds and the creatures that can be found there. Are they written from our sub conscious to encourage us to look within once more, so that we can look out with eyes that can see.

It's funny, we know that to really engage with our world and our outdoors, we need to fully use our senses, but once we manage to do that, we almost need to abandon that knowledge in order to look (hear, smell, touch and taste) past those limitations and see what is within and without. Maybe then we can begin to understand why we are here and what our purpose on this planet, here and now is, or was and what it may become in this life or the next, wherever.

Buddha in his search for enlightenment initially tried to disconnect himself from his senses, before realising that wasn't the way and looked to experience the world through them even more, and then looking past them as we have been doing.

....

To find one potential answer to that question we should look at our children. Have you ever just sat and just watched them play, they have no limiting beliefs, if they can think or imagine it then it should be possible. Sometimes they will just build a structure, sometimes they will fly like a bird or a dragon or maybe even the wind. Sometimes they become animals, princesses or magical creatures, they will re-enact a story they have been told, or seen on the television or just imagined for themselves. They just concentrate on the world around them as it is right 'now'.

They sometimes even have full blown conversations with imaginary friends (as we like to think, but maybe they are real in another reality), or will go and do things out of character, become of afraid of something for no apparent reason, or at least a reason that we as adults, so called, can't perceive.

I have more than once heard it said that children would make the best entrepreneurs. And the reason for that is simple. If they can think it or imagine it then it is possible and they will just do it. The thought that something is impossible doesn't compute or register. They have no boundaries, almost no fears, (we are born with only two fears, fear of loud noises and falling) and they certainly don't make judgements of themselves or others.

Children are children and they are the same the world over, whatever culture, race, creed, nationality, or community they are born into. They just do what they do, are what they are, similarly to all the life we see in our outdoors, or to a large extent the pets we have in our homes. That as I mentioned previously is exactly what all the creatures of our world do, they just get on with the nature of what they are...

If we look at the way children are 'brought up' and nurtured in different cultures, such as those we have discussed here, we might start to explain why different cultures have the different beliefs and strengths and difficulties that they do.

....

It might just be the way different cultures look at themselves and the way they look outward and look to connect with the world around them. Those communities that acknowledge the interconnectedness of all things, animal, vegetable and mineral are part of a greater whole. That knew that the land around them could provide everything they needed as long as they lived in tune with it and didn't try to adjust it for their own ends for more than their basic needs. One only has to look at the way of life of a north American Indian or the mountain communities in Tibet, they knew by long association with their homelands how to live within them, when to harvest whatever was their main food crop, when to stockpile it, how to use it completely, so that there was little, if any waste product. Leave no sign you were there when you leave.

Unconsciously, or innately, the energy transfer was understood and within their spiritual beliefs acknowledged. It was only when the invading 'civilised' cultures invaded that they began to experience hunger and starvation on a scale previously unseen when their connection and access to their ancestral homes that difficulties began to be experienced. More recent examples would be the Indians in the nineteenth century and the Tibetan tribesmen in the twentieth.

You might even say they had a very good understanding of the concept of 'enough'. That is an issue we in the west have little understanding of in many ways. We eat more than we need, we do. Be honest, how often have you found food so enjoyable that you couldn't stop eating until the food ran out. Hunger builds, and gets exaggerated by beautiful smells, we prepare our food to enhance the sensations our taste buds supply to our minds that wallow in that ecstasy. Sometimes that's just because we love the food, but also because we have been brought up to eat all the food on our plate, and we do not get the option to only put on our plates what we want to eat. So we keep eating until our plates are empty. We've been trained to do it.

It maybe because, back far enough in time we would eat all we could because we didn't know when the next meal was coming from, but that's not the case any more for most of us. Not in the modern, western world. We eat because we like to and because we have not given much thought to the concept of enough.

People living on their ancestral lands also a secure belief in an assured future, that maybe it was so certain, they had no worry about it. They knew how to live with the land, and knew that it would look out for them.

....

The same process occurs in much of our world, we strive for more money than a man can use. Strive for promotion at work, the next step up in mobile phone technology, a bigger car and a bigger house. And when we've got all that we tend to push on for the next thing, never satisfied. Having long ago forgotten what it is to have enough. And on top of all that we live in a society that allows us to have it all now and not pay for it until later. We are never full. We become fat, physically and mentally. Where are we transferring all that energy now?

In fact if we look at the world around us there are so many lessons we can learn. Rarely does anything seem to be in a hurry unless it's the act of catching food, trees grow so slowly we can't see it, they have a heartbeat that is so slow we can barely perceive it, let alone see it. Birds fly at the most economical speed in the most economical fashion, and often don't even leave their perch unless they need to. Cows move slowly, usually at the pace they can eat the volume of fodder they need. Waves roll up and down the beach effortlessly. Even bird song is never a hurried event. Everything has a natural order and pace to it. On the occasion that rain becomes torrential, or wind gets up to gale force and tides hammer away at sea defences it is only for a relatively short duration. Not even our natural world can keep up an enforced pace or volume for long. Everything blows through. There's a natural beginning, middle and, ultimately, end to all things. It's cycles again. Somehow, it is only man that has a need to keep pushing in the opposite direction.

In fact, if we could learn to be more flexible in our attitudes, we would be far better at dealing with the unexpected difficulties that strike us from time to time. Take a look at the palm tree on the beach taking a battering in the storm, the top of the tree can bend almost to the ground if necessary to absorb the impact of a storm, and what is even more amazing, is the size of root ball that actually keeps the tree upright. Occasionally a storm is so severe, that a tree will come crashing to the ground, whether due to the storm or other infirmity, take a look at the root ball and compare that to the size of the tree. The size of the root is always small in comparison to the size of the tree. It is the flexibility that keeps the tree upright. The tree always plays to its strengths, even though it is likely that it doesn't know it is doing it.

Have you ever had to walk down a slippery slope? If you have tried to be especially careful and check every step and look for support the whole way, there is every chance you will fall. Conversely, if you took a moment to check for obstacles and just went at a natural, if uncontrolled pace, but just looked to steer your path and 'go with the flow', there is every chance you would get to the bottom safely and in one piece. You need a plan, but then you need to go with it and let the momentum sustain you. You may still fall, but the damage will be less. There is a natural order to all things.

You will also notice that there is only one creature on the planet that continually makes judgements about everything, itself personally, the people known and associated to it, people in their country, people in the world in general, it's place in the world. In fact, where it's world was in the solar system, until Science, 'god bless it', proved we were wrong, but many people took some convincing even then. Figured it out yet? Yes, us, human beings. You need to have a certain amount of ego to live, but many of us have taken it to excess, often without realising it. And let's face it, no matter how important we are, or would like to think we are, we are not really that important in the great scheme of things. The world will carry on when we've self-destructed or imploded, or whatever...

………………………………………………………..

Even natural disasters are a part of natural cycles or are exaggerated by mans behaviour. Building houses on a flood plain whilst not making suitable diversions for the water that used the plain when the river could not contain it or changing a lifestyle that evolved with a traditional culture for example, we've already discussed the American Indians and the hill tribes of Tibet. Or even in the scientifically 'advanced' cultures we enjoy in the west that keep reducing the habitats of bees. The bees that pollinate the food we need to eat, or the food that the animals we eat, eats. Why would we do that? But we do. Having become so removed from the natural cycles that maintain us on this earth and having such a desire for things that we don't need or wanting more than we need. Turning nature into a commodity. We trade connectivity for greed and ego.

The message, if we can call it so, from our world is obvious is we just choose to use all our senses. The world is for the most part in a state of calm, absorbing the excesses of weather and for that matter, manmade damage pretty quickly in the scheme of things. Any Survey of our local area will reveal signs of this ability to heal the scars of our behaviours. Even concrete is dispensed with, with ease. As natural friction begins the make cracks and indentations on the surface of any material, they will fill with water and debris. Very soon mosses and the like will begin to grow, followed by plants that can grow very quickly without great levels of nutrients or water, Buddleia, cow parsley or hogweed for example. These are plants you will see on building sites. If the site is exposed, they will be short, but as soon as shelter becomes evident then they will gain height and shelter that plants around them. It is only a short time before insects and animals will then follow. As temperatures fall then the water that fills cracks will expand as it freezes due to the change of density that water goes through at 4°C. The concrete, if that is what is there, then cracks and decays, more soil fills the space and so more soil, and then more aggressive planting also takes hold. Evidence of our transgressions is still there but quickly becomes hidden. A metaphor for the long-term effects of our arrogance and greed. A lesson for those that look.

And look, some of us do. Because if the lesson is learnt we can use this knowledge and make good on the activities that ultimately we have a need to engage in. Locally, we have Samphire Hoe, a very recent Nature Reserve, a country Park no less. The newest part of the British Isles and an amazing testament to what man and nature can achieve when we work in harmony. Four point nine million cubic meters of chalk marl were dug out of the ground during the construction of the channel tunnel. The site was selected, the massive restraining walls that surround the site were built of steel and reinforced concrete and the created lagoon was filled with the chalk. The area was landscaped, and the existing hills, pools and paths installed, the ground was prepared for chalk meadow down and is home to many species of planting including the Rock Samphire that gives the site it's name, along with the word Hoe which is a piece of land that sticks out into the sea.

An amazing testament to what can be achieved when mankind utilises the strength and abilities of our natural world and works in partnership with nature rather than fighting against it.

AWESOME.

....

What is really special though is the fact that all these great works can happen on many different scales. We discussed above how this can happen on a worldwide stage above with the principle of Gaia, our world as a self-sustaining organism. Or nationally, and each country in this world has differing levels of success but will ultimately work best if we could only agree on issues like the survival of mankind and the world we live on. Seems a no brainer to me.

At a more local level, with examples of decay such as at our abandoned coal mines and the associated workings, nature always reclaims when we are gone. For most of these scales of managements we must rely on the organisations we can join that lobby the decision makers for our survival, the RSPB, Greenpeace or other international bodies, as well as those that actually make up the governments that we elect to make decisions for us. And often they have tracts of land they manage on our behalf, Nature reserves, Areas of outstanding natural beauty or Sites of Special Scientific Interest.

But there is one scale of land preservation, culture, and value we have almost complete control over and that is our own gardens. We can make them havens of beauty, that stimulate our all our senses, that enrich us and fill our lives with life. That instil in us a sense of peace and calm and balance that deep down we know is inherent to our inner peace and contentment. That connects us to our world, allows us to connect, re connect and assess all that we do, and how to address those things that are beyond our control.

There are approximately 23 million gardens in the UK, approximately 460% more area than all the National Nature Reserves according to the National Survey of Homes in the UK from 2001/2. Can you imagine if every garden was managed for wildlife and personal spiritual happiness? And then not just in the UK, but in the whole world. If we all just helped ourselves, spiritually that is, not materially.

So, we are best able to absorb these major events in our life if we are at peace as nature is and also intended for us to be, for most of the time. At peace and in balance. In all aspects of our existence, Naturally, spiritually, physically, mentally and nutritionally. Consciously. Behaviourally. First, we must look at ourselves, and in that, honestly. Remember you can't hide from yourself. Ever!

How you do that will depend on you. And no solution will ever be right for everybody. I am no psychologist, but I know that in the first instance I am responsible for me and my happiness. No one else is and I will not put that responsibility solely in the hands of anyone else. To be of use to anyone else I have to be at peace. To receive and radiate energy in a positive manner as often as possible. And be able to weather the storms that affect my life as constructively as possible. Don't carry anger for example that isn't yours.

It takes a long time to work this out. I wrote down large parts of this process for me in 'the three year pond', not realising what the book was until I had finished it. I now know fully that the process was far from finished when the book was published. Chapter 10 discusses my need to change my relationship with alcohol and the ease of making difficult decisions when you are ready to make them.

....

We have discussed at length above about the fact that life, whether natural or manmade, will put obstacles of myriad and complex natures, in front of us, the choice is only how we deal with these things and look for the learning in all of them. We can control three things and three things only. What we think, what we say and what we do. Everything else we must accept. And then act accordingly.

Now whilst we are thinking about the 'things' we have control over it is useful to acknowledge that even the senses we use to navigate our way around the world we live in is again basically a use of energy, as ever unconscious use of energy.

If we take sight and sound as the most obvious means we personally use energy to perceive our world. Light is a form of electromagnetic energy, it's kinetic, or movement energy, the movement of photons. It's incredibly fast too, nothing moves faster, that we know of. If you are unsure about this, have a look at a jet fighter plane next time one flies over you and then notice where the sound appears to be coming from. You will notice it the sound appears to be coming from behind the plane. This is because sound moves much slower than light. The reason you've never noticed this before is because most things you see and hear are so close the difference is not detectable. Perspective again... Incidentally light can travel through a vacuum, if it couldn't, we wouldn't be able to see in space. And the wave form is called longitudinal, but can't pass through a solid and is blurry through a liquid.

Sound is a transverse wave that passes through a solid, liquid or gas. It's a vibration and most easily visualised by imagining the string on a guitar, if you pluck the string it vibrates. Unlike light energy it can't pass through a vacuum. Incidentally, this was one of the reasons why the strapline for the movie Alien was, 'in space no one can hear you scream!'.

The Qur'an is in Arabic and Muslims believe its message is strongest when read and then heard aloud in the language it was originally transcribed. Indeed, reading and thus hearing words, utilising two forms of energy is likely to increase long term memory, and the brain of course uses a third form of energy, electrical.

If thus follows that you should be careful as to what you say as words have the power to affect the people around you that hear them in more ways than the words you actually use. The words you read also have vibration, but as you can now see it's with a different form. And come to that the words you think, before or after you have said them have a different form of energy again. They all travel in different ways and will also affect what you get, or perceive, or wish for. It's going to extremes, but maybe we should be careful as to watch we watch and listen too, because the inputs we receive affect the way we think and the way we think will affect what we say and that will affect what we get. An easy example of the power of words is just how easily they can be used to drive someone to anger, so they can be used to drive someone to love...

If we blindly sing along to catchy tunes maybe we should monitor what we listen too, if we sing about not finding love, then maybe that's the reality we will attract. If we have a diet of gory horror movies they will also have an effect on the way we think too. There have been many cases of misguided individuals acting out the examples they have perceived to be inspirational from movies.

Again, without energy there would be no conversation.

We just need to keep our perspective realistic!

Chapter Three.

Centres, Chakras, and Auras

This is a book about energy primarily. It veers left and right quite frequently, but at it core is energy which underpins everything, one way or another.

The word meditation has been bandied about quite a bit too.

Meditation has been described in many ways and with many purposes, to quieten the chatter of a busy mind, to achieve connection to a world our bodies have forgotten they are a part of, to find an inner peace, or a sense of the divine, however we may perceive that to be.

However, to me, it's all those these and more. Many times when meditating I feel my body come alive, buzzing as if channelling something that may be energy or similar. Not as gravity defying or spectacular as the quickening at the end of 'Highlander', the movie, (remember that?). But almost similar in a way. Now I know what you're thinking at this point. Nutter, right? Those that already meditate will likely know what I'm saying here, but it's definitely real to me, a connection, or as I said channelling something. And it is intoxicating whilst at the same time not addictive in the least. How is that?

So what can it be? There's only one answer that fits the bill for me. Energy. But that then raises another question for me. Where is it coming from and where is it going? Everything I read or experience tells me it is coming from the universe and going to ground, but I don't know, and my experience doesn't give me any answers. It could just as easily be emanating from the ground and heading to the universe. But I'm not even sure about that, it could be coming from another source, arriving in me, and leaving in all directions, like light from a globe. Or it could be the reverse of that. I could be a portal. Really? I don't know, but it's all possible, after all if it is energy we are talking about here, it is capable of a lot of different things as we already know. Does it relate to any of the experiences described in the trunk of this book?

Certainly the days when energy seems to be flowing freely tend to be days of achievement. Is that because of that energy or just the greater ability of my mind that day, or it purely belief that I am following my path to destiny?

If it is energy, then it follows that some attention should be paid in this text to chakras and auras. Both topics or contexts go back in Hindu scripture for many hundreds, if not thousands, of years. The word chakra is Sanscrit for wheel, and chakras are the energy centres within the body. An aura is the various energy fields that surround our bodies.

Now, here's the juxtaposition of all this for me. As I have stated above, I meditate, quite a lot, and I know, absolutely, there is movement of something, which is most likely energy. I don't question it, I know it. I know within myself, due to continued practice and experience. And it therefore follows that centres, chakras and auras must exist. I am still victim to my western upbringing in many respects, but also the fact that many of the people I have met that talk about and use the words chakra and aura tend to be a little, 'airy fairy', lost in the hippy world, or condescending know all's. Which doesn't help! 'Your aura is blocked', 'you won't experience any thing you're blocking'. At which point they walk away, or look at me pompously, before I have had a chance to reply. "I'm here, help me to understand', or say, 'why is that?'

The well-meaning elite. It's even worse than going into a builder's merchants and not knowing the vocabulary. You ask for a fence post, and they say, '4 by 4 at 2.4'. At least when you say to them, 'yeah right', and ask them to explain in English they do.

I should say that not all practitioners of meditation who talk about chakras and auras are like that in the least, it's always the exception to any rule that stands out in your mind.

As I said, that's a wrong generalisation. I started my meditation practice at a book writing course and Sharon, White Elk Woman, was not like that at all, and nor was Angela, who introduced me to Twin Hearts Meditation and nor is Nam, who runs the online 'twin hearts' meditation I attend on a regular basis. In fact it may be due to the three of them that I find myself bold enough to put this chapter together at all.

That and the fact that the 'twin hearts meditation' has been put through the rigours of scientific investigation and found to have a positive effect on those that practice it. It still needs more research, but it is reassuring that the needs of those of us in the west are starting to validate what those of eastern practices have said all along. I look forward to the day when both practices merge together. Wouldn't that be just the most amazing event ever...

So up this point the only Auras I would have been prepared to discuss without contempt would have been the albums by The Mission, not their best, or by Asia, fantastic and seriously overlooked.

Have you ever met someone, known or not and just had a sense that they were in a bad mood, or a good mood, or might be sensitive to your proposal, or worry or concern? I'm sure you have; we all have at some time or another. By this I mean, not exchanged a word or a look, just known. This would have been due to an aura. We all emit energy, all the time, and we can receive it too. It's likely then that that energy can alter depending on how we feel, or more importantly the way people around us feel. As well as affect the way they feel.

Those people who are empathetic, are said to channel this energy more strongly than others. My wife works quite often with those whose lives have been disrupted by illness and are experiencing great emotional trauma and there's no doubt about it, I can usually tell when she's been working in this capacity. She will arrive home drained in a way, that a day on her feet hairdressing does not achieve. Emotionally drained, her positivity in need of restoration. I leave her to herself and wait for her to balance out and engage once more.

That is aural transmission and reception or absorption in extreme. But I think, we have all experienced it to some level.

So, what actually is an aura? An energy field, or several energy fields around us. Reading various texts will describe several layers about the body, the etheric layer, a kind of buffer between the physical body and next layer, the emotional aura, which in turn is surrounded by the mental layer and the soul aura around that.

I have met people that claim they can see auras; I cannot argue with them. But I cannot see auras. Not even when squinting. I want them to exist, it would be so cool, but as I said above there are enough instances of mental and emotional transmission in our lives that cannot be easily explained, but have little proof or explanation, but then this book isn't about proof, but questioning how far we can push our belief of what has to be true even in if it can't be measured, with obviously, what we struggle to believe in too.

And that leads us to Chakras, or Centres.

Chakras are the energy centres in our bodies, where energy is stored and transferred, or used to make our bodies work efficiently. They draw in energy and pump it into our organs. Like any organ in our body, they work at an optimum capacity, but can also be overworked or blocked. They are all connected with some taking on more responsibility than others, but effectively they work as in a large network of sections or divisions. Energy is absorbed from the food we eat, the amount of exercise you do, the environment that surrounds us, and our mental and emotional state, the universe, and the ground. They help us maintain a sense of balance. Also expelling excess energy that we don't need.

Spirituality requires three factors to be in balance, an intelligent mind, a powerful will and drive, and a dynamic body. All can be nurtured by keeping our chakras balanced. If you think about if one of those components is missing, then your effectiveness will be severely reduced. An intelligent mind and a dynamic body, without the will to carry out the brilliant theories, and those brilliant theories will be wasted. Do you remember those school reports that said could do better? Or the difficulties Professor Stephen Hawkins had to overcome because his body was anything but dynamic?

So, energy and Chakras. Depending on the text you read there are varying numbers of them, but most texts refer to seven and briefly we will look at them here.

Usually, they are described from the bottom up, base to crown. But if energy comes to us from the universe to ground, then it makes sense to me to begin at the crown chakra.

The Crown Centre

The Crown Centre, Chakra or Sahasara is at the top of our head, the centre of spiritual consciousness, where energy enters our body When balanced and working effectively helps us to feel connected, calm and at peace with the world. We have compassion and loving kindness at the centre of all our actions. It is triggered by the heart chakra.

When our crown chakra is balanced we use our will effectively to govern our actions and are able to grasp and solve problems quickly. Our power of intuition works well and effectively. If we meditate then the crown chakra gets bigger and attracts more high frequency energy.

Making 'wrong' decisions is an easy to spot sign of our crown chakra being blocked or overworked.

The Ajna Centre

The forehead or Ajna chakra, the 'third eye', found, above the eyes, as said on the forehead. This is the chakra that is responsible for the use of our intellect, understanding of the abstract and control of our emotions. An efficiently functioning Ajna chakra will help you to smile when under pressure and lead others responsibly.

It is here we know truth and learn from all sources of knowledge whether from others, books, or the world of nature around us and focus on what needs to be done.

When well-balanced our ajna chakra will flood the whole of the body with energy.

Not making sense of a situation is a sign of an Ajna chakra out of balance.

The Throat Centre

The throat chakra or Vishuddha is the chakra of purification, communication, creativity and responsibility.

It governs the throat, mouth and all associated organs, as well as those we listen with. It is connected to the sex chakra, and it is this connection that means that often highly creative people have an enlarged sex drive. It is also highly receptive to worry as is often evidenced by people who are worried lose the ability to communicate effectively. Conversely, those who deal with truth and responsibility often communicate well and effectively.

The Heart Centre

Anahata, the heart chakra, is where emotion and intellect meet. Where you choose between the higher ideals of hope, trust, forgiveness, empathy and love over anger, envy, want and impatience.

Connected to the heart, and healing, this chakra must be activated before the crown to achieve soul connection and spiritual development, thus the two chakras are the main focus for the twin hearts meditation I have mentioned several times.

Balance is essential, an overactive, or poorly performing heart chakra will have a serious effect on the operation of the heart.

The Power Centre

The power centre, Manipura or solar plexus chakra affects confidence, intelligence, courage, sense of self and justice. Those emotions that are vital but need to be kept in balance to avoid over ambition, self-righteousness or recklessness.

It's also connected to the gastric system, liver, pancreas, intestines as well as the diaphragm and for this has an obvious connection to all other chakras. After all, where does stress have a major habit of showing up?

The Will Centre

The will centre, sex or sacral chakra, or Svadhishthana, a heathy love of self, happiness, creativity, desire and sexuality. A sense of belonging.

A place to remove waste material, literally and metaphorically. Connection to liver, kidneys, and spleen. And obviously to the sexual organs.

The need to keep this chakra operating with balance is clear...

The Base Centre

And the bottom is the basic, basal or root chakra called Muladhara in sanskrit, the feeling of being safe and living without fear. Commitment to the task and feeling energetic come from here.

The place to start when healing any other chakra. Also the chakra to boost when looking for success, whilst taking care not to over activate which will lead to hyperactivity or possibly insomnia and restlessness. A weak root chakra can lead to depression.

There is an awful lot to think about here and we should be grateful that for the most part they are all in balance and operating as intended for most of the time, but it is useful to look at how they are connected in a useful and realistic context.

So, all the way through this book we keep coming back to energy. And that affects everything. Just think, you can't have an emotion without having a thought. Think about it (SIC), you can't. You can't be unhappy unless you perceive you have something to be unhappy about. Both thoughts and emotions require energy. Positive thoughts are high energy and negative thoughts are low energy.

If you are happy, you tend to be bouncy and enthusiastic. Your body feels light. Conversely, when you are sad or unhappy you will have a tendency to be lethargic and have to work hard to even drag yourself off the sofa. This is positive and negative energies at work.

Both are contagious. Because we focus on them, and then they build. If we are angry, this sits in the Solar Plexus chakra. Enough of it and it creates a dam and then energy cannot flow. It will then get transferred to our liver, or our digestive system and we often cease to feel hunger. It can also give us backache. If we hold onto it for long enough it could even cause diabetes.

How do we clear the solar plexus chakra? The first thing to do as mentioned before is move. Pick yourself up and go for a walk. Biophillia. This will activate the basic chakra. What do you want? Plan to make it happen, activate the high frequency energies. This will activate the ajna chakra. Think about how it will feel, activate the lower frequency energies, the ajna chakra will then activate the throat chakra and the heart chakra, and then do something that you have planned, book some time off or go and see friends, whatever. Now the crown chakra is working too. Anger blocks these connections, but you've taken action and started clearing the blockages.

If you don't act, then great ideas will be lost because of procrastination and frustration. Do not let anyone or anything unbalance you because it will block the connections between the energy centres.

Like the cliché says, 'the universe does not give you what you want, it gives you what you are'. Remember the law of attraction and the law of resonance. It is all connected. Energy, thoughts, and desires. Words have frequencies, we must use them with care. Replace words of low energy with those of high energy. Think about it, which words make you feel good? Use them when you feel yourself coming down. That will help you dispel unhelpful thoughts and energies and help your chakras help you.

Maybe the secret here is 'to go with it', whether you believe it or not, because belief is often the secret to success with anything. If you can't prove chakras don't exist then utilise the belief, because we know energy exists and there must be something channelling and utilising it within us. In a way that boosts the chemical transitions we know and believe exist.

Now you might be thinking. 'Yeah, the organs operate because the brain tells it too'. And you would be right, but everything needs energy, and energy has to travel around too. Some of it travels through nerve systems and some of it transfers from chakra to chakra. Everything is connected and, in more ways, than we can probably imagine...

To go

A journey through, that's what it is

A route down, experiencing the heavy

Enduring, bearing

Pushing onward, pushing through

Wait for a moment, a trigger

That sparks the light

That draws you up

Where breath comes more easily

And the weight slides away

Emerging once again, celebrate cycle

That we only go down, so that

We can celebrate the light.

Part two. We branch out.

So, what can we see if we look?

Sometimes it's just being observant.

Sometimes it's actively going to look.

Chapter Four.

The world is different on the water, or the choices we make.

The world is different on the water. The rest of the world recedes and somehow becomes more distant, everyday sounds become further off, the noise of traffic and the sounds of people fade away.

The rush and general hustle and bustle of the lives we have created for ourselves become almost a distant memory. There are no deadlines, or targets to meet, just the gentle relentless pace of the river, all we have to do is delicately keep ourselves pointed in the right direction, remembering not to over steer and so keep ourselves on whatever is the right track for us.

You see the parallels come easily, but right now let's just focus on the river, and the inspiration for this part of my story, and I suppose to do that it makes sense to go back a few years.

It was 2016 I think, high and heady after our wonderful walk along the West Highland Way, My son, Ross, and I had discovered we'd accidentally walked a section of the North Downs Way, the recent name given to the Pilgrims Way, as used by those making the Pilgrimage to Canterbury many years ago. It seemed only natural then to make a plan to walk the complete trail, which we duly did.

The story of that walk will have to wait for another day, but suffice it to say, one day's walking became a real feat of endurance and when we eventually finished, Ross' feet were ruined and as much as he wanted to continue walking the next day, we had to accept the inevitable and call for help. The rest of the walk would have to wait for another day.

Have you ever found yourself at home when you should have been on holiday? It is the most strange and surreal experience. To be at home when you should not be there, to not get involved in a project, because that's what you do when you're at home and not working or getting dragged back into work because you're self-employed and work is based at home. Especially when your still fit and healthy but your holiday mate is laid up.

We needed an activity that didn't need much use of feet but was stimulating and could be powered by upper body strength. Rummaging around on the internet we found a local company called Canoe Wild that hired out canoes on the River Stour and they were reasonably priced, so we booked and off we went.

Whilst all the benefits of a river were very evident on that trip, when you have a teenager on board everything must be done as fast as possible, Ross paddled like a dervish and my role became one of steering. Now we are already getting back onto the theme of parallels again, think about it, come on...

So, fast forward to now and I'm about to take you, on a physical and metaphorical trip down the river, with our paddle, both real and imagined, firmly in hand.

The first thing you notice on a river, as I said above is that the rest of the world recedes and your reality becomes the pace of the water, the direction of the water, the sound of water, what's in the water, what's above the water, what's either side of the water, but mostly, the water itself, after all its keeping you afloat in your boat. And don't forget your boat, that's keeping you dry, as well as making it easier to go in the direction you may have chosen.

It is my wife's birthday, and this trip is a surprise, we have had a few river trips, some with my son, who as I said, likes to do everything at breakneck pace and a couple of trips in a gondola, both in Venice on honeymoon and recently on our wedding anniversary in Canterbury. So, I thought an enjoyable paddle along the Stour would be idyllic; and it was, but like on any journey, there are elements that you cannot control that definitely have a huge impact on the success of the day. As I told you in the last book, for our son's wedding day all the elements lined up just perfectly, and we were just as lucky on our Wedding Day, after days of rain, the sun came out, it was hot enough for our wedding suits and dresses, but not so hot that we all baked, and that allowed us to use the inside and outside of the venue for all the different elements that make up a wedding just as we wished.

And so it was today, the rain the day before had been torrential, enough that in half an hour the pond in our garden filled by an inch, and the day after the rain just persisted as an English summer rain will tend to do, but on my wife's birthday it was 24 °C, warm enough for t shirts and summer dresses, but not so warm that any exertion was exhausting.

As with any journey, a little care must be taken on departure, going from a stable platform to one that moves requires a little care and technique. Sit on the jetty, put your feet in the boat and rotate your bottom into position. Grab your pack lunch and you're ready to go. Then you become part of the motion and it all becomes natural. No sea sickness here. As you leave the docking station the first thing you have to do is get your head around a slightly different steering system to the one we are used to, otherwise, as many do, all you do is visit each bank on a regular basis. Infuriating and embarrassing. You must also realise that as soon as you input a direction change, the boat will continue on that path for a while.

So, paddling on the left, to go right, and on the right to go left, and gently so, trying not to over steer, you, or in this case us, head off downstream. In a boat, of course, the engine room is in the front, and you steer from the rear. It's not long before vigorous paddling gains forward momentum, and then its more about simply steering, everything becomes gentler and the whole pace becomes well 'just as it should be' and your consciousness begins to expand away from the boat.

At first, just to the water itself, lapping and slapping and wobbling as water does, and how the boat reflects this, as it must, after all we are afloat and the water along with the life around it, becomes our world. Then you look down and see the water plants both on and below the surface, all fronds heading in one direction, after all they are slave to the tide, as are we. Buttercups, rushes and lilies, providing a home to the myriad of creatures that live in a river, either for some or all of their lives, the larvae or nymph stages of diving beetles, damselflies and dragon flies, snails like the wandering or pond snails to name but a few.

The water being clear, indicates a good natural balance of plant and animal life, the flora and fauna and a stable riverbed. Further upstream as the tide is stronger the water becomes murky as the water is driven tidally, disturbs the bottom making anything unattached move uncontrollably.

Inevitably, especially when the pace is slow your tummy demands attention and from our pack lunch, I pass my wife a strawberry.

And then you see the banks, rising from the water, often blocking out sound and view, often elder. Thought by many as a weed, a plant to be cut down and removed whenever it raises its head, but here left to do its own thing as nature intended, white this time of year and perfect for white wine as my father used to make. Late in the year full of red berries, a much nicer red in my opinion, full and fruity. We have one in the garden at home, carefully placed and pruned to be a colourful addition to our own small take on paradise.

Crack willow is common, both on the bank and at the edge of fields behind it, large and weeping as described by poets and romantics in equal measure. And while it is a beautiful addition to any riverside visage, it is of little use to any creature, the leaves being very small, long and thin and offering little shelter. Anything trying to make a living there getting washed away as soon as it rains, maybe this is part of the reason there are so many in our countryside, or maybe it's just the romantics.

Periodically we see a dog rose, the simple flowers white and just kind of 'pink blush', standing out from the background of green behind them. Somehow these ancestral roses have a simple beauty far greater than the cultivated complexity and bold colours of the genetically 'enhanced' flowers that fill our gardens these days. The bees seem to prefer them too, there's certainly plenty here, white tail and red tail bumbles quietly going about their business.

It's then that you notice other movement too, there are several species of damselfly, blues and greens and browns. But the most spectacular, and I love them, are the banded demoiselle. The males are an iridescent purply black, magnificent in itself, but what really makes them stand out are the purply black ovals on each wing. In flight it doesn't take much to imagine fairies and it's only another small leap of the imagination to think these stunning little insects may well be where all the stories began. When our ancestors first started trying to make sense of the world in which they lived, and try to get some sense of where they fitted in. After all as I mentioned, there's got to be something more 'gluing' all this together other than just fluke and accident.

Then you realise that there's more than just one, they are in two's mostly and sometimes there are others flying around too. Watching them becomes hypnotic as they skim the surface dancing about and land on anything floating in the water, or the grasses and reeds on the banks, one to her great pleasure lands on my wife's hand. She has a strawberry in the other and frustratingly can't take a picture. So magical are they that we try to film them for posterity. Its then that we understand why there are no great videos on you tube, or anywhere else for that matter, it's not an easy thing to do. We have many videos of reeds and floating jetsam, sometimes a tail, the abdomen as they take flight. It's almost as if they know.

With the sun delightfully warming your back as you float downstream it's so easy to let your consciousness wander, but the river demands that you keep a modicum of attention on the task at hand or you'll find yourself in the bank. The phone goes and my wife answers it, keeping us centre stream requires less effort as her enthusiastic steering eases. We see cows that look up, nonchalantly, from their chewing as we pass. Looking up we see jays, colourful crows flying from bank to bank, all pinks and blues, whites and black, and their mischievous cousin's magpies; all singles, I hope the rhyme is not true. As we pass a lake there are common terns, one sitting on an old post from when the area used to be home to a colliery and the other flying like a stuka dive bomber, up and down as it fishes for its dinner. Magnificent. And then there are two herons, one stood typically in the water, the other dive bombing it and making a skwarking noise, never heard that before. Later it settles, although each time we get close it alights and flies a hundred yards or so, before settling once again, until once again we disturb it, and the cycle is repeated.

My wife reaches out her hand behind her, an unspoken request for another strawberry, the perfect food for a trip on the river.

It is at this point that I remember that Paul, a friend of mine mentioned last week that there seems to be very few swallows, martins, and swifts in our skies. I know swifts arrive much later than the others but even so…. I would normally expect to see swallows swooping down just above the surface of the water, hunting for the insects that make up their diet, but I haven't seen one today, or much at all recently though.

There's an oak, magnificent long-lived trees, with unmistakable leaf shapes, it's branches stretching far out over the water. Magnificent for wildlife of all kinds, there is as I recall over 150 types of organism making a living out of an oak tree.

I'm hopeful that we might see a kingfisher, not common, and shy, but unmistakable with that iridescent blue that seems to streak passed when you do see them, but not today. It is always a good day when you see a kingfisher.

There are marsh harriers here, but none show today. Magnificent raptors that are the masters of slow flight, and hen harriers too, but they go north for the summer, over wintering here. Their numbers are down, they are still unpopular with game keepers, allegedly…

We do though hear a cuckoo, the first of the year for me. Magnificent avian parasites that they are. Taking as much care of their young as many insects. 'Plonk' an egg in a nest and leave the host to bring up the chick. Seems to work well enough. Cuckoo calls are fewer these days, but I don't think it's the chick raising technique that is responsible, well unless the hosts, warblers usually, numbers are down.

There's a splash, a small fish jumps clear of the water, probably means there's a pike about, there are no fisherman here.

All to soon we go passed the moorings, and because it's a Sunday the boats are full of people, most probably down for the weekend, most are just relaxing, some are looking after their beloved boats, after all unlike a car, no one buys a boat because they have too, I imagine they just 'get it'. But it also means that shortly we'll pass under the road bridge and that means our trip is almost over.

But hey, hang on a minute, that's not true, we're somewhere in the middle, so it can't be over. Do you remember at the beginning of the chapter I said there were so many parallels? Well, that's what this section of book is about. Let's just think about this for a minute.

As we have already mentioned, whilst we like to feel we are in control of our own destiny, there has to be something that plots our course, doesn't mean we have to take that path, but usually it proves best and most rewarding when we do. A river is the perfect analogy of that.

Most of us are living very fast paced lives, and often we don't have control of what happens around us, we can change the pace of our lives in the long term by making a few very important well thought out decisions. But most importantly, even if our lives are fast paced, we don't have to have minds that are operating at that pace unless we choose to let them. There are ways of doing that and once again a river is the perfect analogy of that.

Plotting the course that is right for us, working out how to get there and not overreacting to situations is vital to having a fulfilled life, whatever you wish it to be. That's pretty simple too... A river is the perfect analogy of that and like a river you need to keep going.

Having the patience to realise that everything will come to you in time, if as I said you plot your course carefully is very difficult, but there is a natural order to things to that too. I spent many a time with my son as he grew up helping him have patience when all his mates had everything 'now!' 'It's all coming mate...'

Again, a river...... do you get the picture?

Taking stock of what is around you, and stock is the right word, for it is all yours, you just don't own it, is vital. The ancestors of just about every culture that has been on this planet has had a far better understanding of this world and has been far more in touch with it than we are. A river is the perfect place to do that, and we'll focus on some of the little miracles we can bring into our lives too.

And if we have any kind of empathy for our world and the natural order of our world and where we fit into it, then we have an inkling into the term 'spiritually' and ultimately that's what this book is about. A river is great place to do that, especially if when we can't get into a church.

Until recently there was one part if my life that I 'regretted', because I didn't understand the 'why', well now I do, and for me that was absolutely major. Actually, I didn't figure that out on a river, but hey, often it's the exceptions that are the most memorable.

Chapter Five.

The world beckons.

Experiencing the reality, the 5 senses

Introduction

So, we have already mentioned that we explore our world through our 5 senses. It makes sense then to study them with a little more focus. Many of us naturally take them for granted, but if any of them stopped working our lives would be very different. Can you imagine life without any of them? Still, first, let's think a little about how lucky we are to have a planet at all...

And we are lucky. Incredibly lucky when we actually think about it, to be here at all. And by here, I mean not only with an awesome planet to live on in the first instance, but to actually exist ourselves! At all.

Have you thought about it? Even wondered slightly? Arrogantly I'll suggest you probably haven't. Maybe in passing during a science fiction movie maybe, but that's probably about it. I suspect you probably just take all this for granted.

But, and it is a huge BUT, when you think about it, there are probably millions of planets out there and we happen to have one that's suitable for us to live and exist, on. Just one, as far as we know, and we have looked at quite a few. Now, take that a step further. That makes us totally insignificant, when you think as to just how big this world, solar system and universe is, and how many universes there might be. So park up your ego right there. But also, so very important as a species (along with every other species that is), because the likelihood is that there are very few planets, if there are any others, anywhere else, anywhere, that manage to arrange atoms in such a way that life can become the living breathing thinking things that we are, or like to think we are, so we are actually very important and at the same time very fragile, individually and as life at all. If we lost the fight for our lives and the lives on our planet it is just possible life would cease to exist anywhere.

How then did life manage to begin here? Why might that be? Well briefly it's because of several (many) factors, but it boils down to four things, the first is positioning, the second, our planet is made of the right stuff, thirdly we're one of two and forth, a huge dose of good luck, or just great timing.

Our sun is just the right size, and we are in the only amenable position from it. Venus is too hot and Mars to cold. It's burning at the right speed, as a species we are very intolerant of temperature change. We like to think we love the sun, but if it's too hot we become gibbering idiots' way too quickly and that's pretty similar experience with extreme cold too.

Second our planet has a great composition, the core is full of molten lava and stuff. This keeps us warm and releases lots of gasses into our atmosphere and helps form the ozone layer which keeps cosmic stuff out and helps to keeps heat and oxygen and other stuff in; and keeps all that stuff contained and at the right temperature, so we can exist. Nowhere else has that!

Thirdly, we have a partner in crime in all this, the moon. Really a planet in itself. And before we get to the timing bit, it kicks in here too. As you've probably heard we got knocked into a few years ago by a very big rock, a meteorite, and in that collision some of our rock and that of the meteorite got dislodged, went into space, passed through our atmosphere and the ozone layer and with the help of some gravity formed the moon. The moon keeps us stable, and we all need a little stability. The moon keeps our rotation stable, so we don't get into a spinning top wobble and things stay nice and even, days the same length (in total), weeks the same length, we can tolerate months and day/night ratios that change in length, as long as that change stays the same. Imagine living far to the north of the Northern hemisphere where in winter its almost night, all day and in summer, daytime all day.

And fourth, timing. If you think about all the creatures that have lived and become extinct on this planet and the things that must have happened to cause life to evolve, formation of the atmosphere, the ability to reproduce, crawl out of the seas, crawl back in for some creatures. Learn to move about, harder on land than in water, ice ages, meteorite impacts and even our own tendency to self-destruct, the fact that we are here at all in the shape (form) we are in should be celebrated. We should be shouting it out from the rooftops.

There are few creatures that survived intact throughout all that in largely the same form. Crocodiles and dragonflies are two.

If that meteorite had not impacted, then dinosaurs would probably still be roaming the earth and mammals would probably have never got started at all. Never mind the effect it had on the atmosphere....

So, the fact that we have a world to experience sensually is just awesome, fantastic and all those wonderful superlatives that mankind is so good at, is almost beyond belief, but here it is. And in that reality, we should make every effort to understand, interact, harmonise, experience and enjoy it as often as our busy minds will let us.

And on that note, we should explore what should surely be the content of this text, the five senses. You see once upon a time not so long ago we were a part of the big outside world that in recent times we have isolated ourselves from. We relied on those senses to keep us alive, alert, and aware of what was around us so that we could survive and enjoy our world. We had a better connection and empathy for the environment or habitat we live in, not because we chose to, but rather because it chose us and in doing so provided us with everything we actually needed to survive. In short, the outdoors is primal to us, it's part of our DNA.

Having existed, indeed evolved alongside the outdoors, we knew how to look after and nurture our nature, after all it kept us alive and had done for thousands of years. We knew what to eat and when, which creatures were needed to keep other creatures and plants alive and healthy. And knew intuitively when the balance was out and what to do about it. I suspect most of us couldn't survive if all our supermarkets shut, well not for long anyway.

To regain all that knowledge would take a long time and many would argue, 'what's the point?' Well, I would suggest if we realigned ourselves a little with the magic of the outdoor world, we just might be better, happier people, and whilst it may take a while for our minds to remember I would suggest our bodies remember very well, indeed I would go as far as to say have never forgotten. Which is why, unless you are in a tearing hurry, when you go outside you unconsciously take a deep breath of clean fresh air. Your body remembers.

So, five senses, taste, touch, smell, hearing and sight. All very different and stimulating in different ways. One is two way, one triggers memory like no other, and can automatically it seems turn itself on and off at will, one has the ability to stop you in your tracks, yet remove it and the other four heighten very quickly, one keeps your attention longer than the others, and another facilitates conversation so well we utilise it unconsciously but expressly for that purpose. The examples are endless.

It is part of what makes us human. We experience our world sensually. We are no more stimulated than when we are outside. Most of the things that stimulate us indoors we have brought in from the outside. And I mean stimulated, not entertained.

So, with all those superpowers it is difficult to prioritise any of our senses, they affect us so strongly yet we are so blissfully unaware of the effect they have on us on a daily basis to actually focus on each one separately and with as much intensity as possible must be a good thing. After all, as the mindfulness people tell us the more aware we are of 'now' the more life we actually live. We cannot determine how long we have, but we can determine how much of life we experience and that requires awareness and that requires full acknowledgement of our senses which after all give us ultimate contact with our world. And that, maybe, determines our awareness, dare I say it our 'soul'. That thing that makes us more than just the sum of our parts, and there's an awful lot of them. It is our senses that give us the experience that is here and now. Not our actual bodies...

Let me explain, just imagine there is a robot in Jon O Groats in Scotland. You are wherever you are. You are looking at video screens connected to the 'eyes' of the robot, you are hearing from speakers connected to microphones the robot uses for ears, you smell what the robot smells, you sense the wind passing that the robot experiences and you can taste the same air. Your body determines your location, but your senses determine where your soul resides, that thing that gives your body a sense of self, a sense of life, or conscience maybe. Recognise and experience your senses and appreciate them for the amazing, I repeat, amazing reality sensors they are. Try spending a day blindfolded, or with ear defenders on, it is likely you would find life very difficult.

Now having got your attention, there is another thing about our senses that we need to point out. And maybe that's what we are exactly dealing with here, there's a huge difference between, seeing, and actually looking. Or hearing and actually listening. Maybe great

81

examples of this are driving, how many times have you driven along a familiar road, seen the road and the cars or whatever in front of you, only to realise at the end of your journey that you can't remember any of it, sometimes even not remembering that you passed through several villages for example, or having conversation with people and suddenly remembering you haven't listened well enough to remember what the person said. And may have actually answered a question you can't remember.

Context can make a huge difference too, I am as guilty of both examples above as anyone, but when I am in the countryside I am really looking and hearing all the time, I absolutely have to see, hear, smell and quite often touch everything that is there. Maybe I need a text like this for indoors.

And is there a sixth sense, well let's see...

OK I've been wandering again. Senses, where to start, well...

1. Touch

For me, touch has to be the first one. It is the only sense that works two ways. You can reach out to touch, but we can feel things touching us too. That's pretty mind blowing. Touch is attributed to receptors in our skin that react to touch of any kind, and they are extremely receptive or sensitive.

They react to temperature in the first instance, it's the sense of touch that tells us to take a layer of clothes off if we are too hot, that loves the beautiful heat in April when we get a little closer to the sun because of our elliptical orbit and our Earth warms up a little. That beautiful heat, intoxicating when we can find a sheltered spot out of the wind that is still cold. The cold that when we feel it's touch makes the hairs on our arms stand up in a desperate attempt to keep us warm, a body skill left over from when we had a lot more hair. An example that shows our bodies remember.

I love the heat from an April sun, warm enough that I feel the energy stimulating me as I sit and soak up those invigorating almost intoxicating rays, utterly different to the stimulation of a cold crisp frosty day, exhilarating in a totally different way. All crisp and refreshing, you feel the heat of the sun, but it's the stillness that goes with it, an island of time. As we crunch through the frozen puddles and walk on ground that for now has lost its squelch and is firm, supporting us as we enjoy its splendour. Both almost fresh and new, but in utterly different ways. And we can distinguish between them unconsciously, just how cool is that! More so if we take a moment to think about it.

Add to that the feel of a gentle breeze across our skin, cooling on a hot day, or just reminding us gently on a cold day that we are alive. And as I mentioned earlier, the freshness we feel as we breathe after an extended period indoors, air so fresh you can taste it, and that is another sense. You feel it touch you all the way down to your lungs and sometimes it makes you shiver and again you feel more alive, as you say 'ohh,' someone just walked over my grave.'

In complete contrast, how we feel when the rain is coming down and the wind is making it horizontal. Many of us at that point head off to the indoors and warmth that we find in our houses, unconsciously we rejoice in the change of stimulations our touch receptors give. We shed clothes and settle back into the cosy warmth of our isolating boxes, maybe unconsciously going back to the beautiful warmth we first felt in the womb and now experience, albeit differently again in the bath, or enjoy sitting in front a crackling wood fire, wood brought in from the outside, or curl up in a duvet as we search for that enveloping feeling that has to begin with touch.

But do you know there is a real argument for fighting against that desire, at least temporarily. Have you ever stayed outside when it's raining? I don't mean getting wet, because as we all know getting wet, unless it is really warm is seriously unpleasant, but staying outside under cover when it's raining is really stimulating. There's an energy in rain, there really is. Even more so when there's thunder and lightning. It's a multi-sensory experience and there will be more about that later. As those large drops plummet from on high and explode on the ground, smaller drops raising high once more before gravity determines their reality and light gets filtered through them making rainbows of various and differing sizes. And when it's warm enough that we take off and run in the rain and feel alive in a way we never thought possible. We just have to let go of our learned sensibilities and enjoy our world freely.

Which leads us back to where I started, touch is a two-way sense. We can also reach out and use any part of our bodies to touch anything we want to. And nature has so many things for us to touch. How often do you take off your shoes and socks and feel the grass beneath your feet, cleansing after the rain or the warmth of bricks after the sun has been out? You can feel the earths energy flow through you when you remove that barrier to sensual experience. Don't get me wrong, nowadays we need our shoes, a lot of the surfaces we have made are unpleasant to feel under our feet, and we like our feet to be soft, certainly they are not as hard as they used to be.

As children we touch everything, almost getting in trouble for touching somethings and we stop touching so that we don't get into trouble. Somethings are unpleasant to touch, no one after all would recommend brushing passed stinging nettles, but the toxins they defend themselves with could also be described as invigorating rather than just painful. After all they are not just defending themselves, but the myriad of beetles and caterpillars that depend on them to survive.

But we also learn, many's the time people have said we must remove the nettles, 'so that our grandchildren don't sting themselves', 'ahh', I say, 'but they'll only do it once'. It's funny though, I only seem to get stung when I don't see them, if I know they are there I can walk through them, even in shorts and not get stung. Has to be something psychosomatic going on there I think. Maybe my sense of touch has a sense of humour. They certainly make you feel alive. Have you noticed how sometimes the stings fade in about twenty minutes and sometimes seem to last for days? Odd.

We touch so many things unconsciously, but if you actually thought about the things you touch again there is a sense of wonder to unlock. People laugh at others who touch trees, but that is just misunderstanding. The differing types of bark are there to discover, silver birch is smooth, often peeling back, the trunks are generally narrow. Often cool to the touch. Now if you compare that to the trunk of a pine tree, deeply ridged and almost sponge like, warm to the touch.

The tough authority of an ash tree trunk or the long-lived abrasive trunk of oak.

Or the silkiness of a rose petal on a sunny day, the stiff smoothness of a holly leaf in adulthood or the pliable nature of the younger leaf. Have you ever emulated Maximus in those opening scenes of Gladiator and run your hand across the roughness of wheat, and compared it to the wispiness of barley?

Touch is also so sensitive we can tell the difference between one and two sheets of newspaper if we put them between our thumb and first finger, that is incredible.

Of course, we mustn't forget one of the most important benefits of touch, much as all the textures we might feel are essential to any fulfilled existence and life itself, we mustn't forget we are pack animals and the greatest bonding experience going has to be a hug. The warmth of a hug from those we love might just be the most important sensual experience we can have. In many cultures a hug is the first embrace made upon meeting, it's just us 'reserved' English, that have begun to refrain. How often have you heard, 'oh, that's so European!" We do at least shake hands.

And many also kiss, especially with our chosen partners, or across the sexes. A statement of togetherness we save it for those special to us generally. And that necessarily close proximity naturally leads on to the next of our senses. Smell.

2. Smell

We receive scents, aromas, whiffs and all things 'hanging' in the air through receptors in our noses.

For many of us smell maybe the least thought about of our five senses. Only ever becoming the subject of conversation when we release unwanted gases ourselves. Always a fit topic for the comedian in all of us. At which all the various changes are worthy of description, 'silent, but deadly', or 'loud and proud!" and all the clichés that go with that act.

But for me the most interesting part of the sense of smell that comes from that act is the ability of our bodies to actually turn off this sense. Have you ever thought about the fact that we only smell these noxious smells for a short period before they 'go' away? The smell itself doesn't, just our ability to receive it. Diffusion (the process by which a smell expands) actually occurs very slowly, smells don't just disappear, just our ability to receive them. Even a walk through a sewer is only smelly for a short time. A colleague used to work for a human sewage company and his vehicle was permeated with the associated aroma, but very soon you would forget about it.

An absolute bonus really, but it's also true for the world's most intoxicating smells. So, it goes without saying we should make sure we have utilised the best ones, because very quickly the only people who will smell them are the people we meet as we travel through our day. We all like to think we smell 'nice', but in case we don't many of us like to enhance our personal aroma.

The success of a date with my favourite lady in times past was mostly determined by a suitor's aroma, fail that 'test' and a second date was an impossibility.

Historically, perfumes were essential for that very reason, and our hygiene wasn't as good as it is now...

Also, considering how we neglect our sense of smell it is very particular, there are so many scents available in our world and so many based on the outside world we have often isolated ourselves from.

Our fresh air sprays represent the smells we love from outside, pine forests, apple orchards, ocean spray or sandalwood. Also, our detergents, bubble baths, deodorants and conditioners, all bringing the outside in, reminding us of a world we were once a part of, or once was a huge part of us.

So, if we go outside and smell these aromas first hand that surely has to be a better stimulant for us to 'wake' up to and feel alive. Often best experienced on a still day, when the wind hasn't had a chance to blow those wonderful smells away. On a summers day when you walk into a flower garden and the scent of roses or apple blossom assaults your noses, stopping you in your tracks as you let the wonder of life permeate your being and you wander in search of other scents to keep your 'fix' at its maximum. Choisias, lavender, jasmine or gardenia. Or of an evening when stocks or honeysuckle will fill the air. We don't just take these flowers indoors because the look pretty.

All of a sudden, the world feels an amazing place in which to be alive.

But it doesn't have to be the scents from a designed and planned garden that will lift the weight off your shoulders. If it's damp then still go outside, even in the middle of winter the smells of our world, woodlands in particular, are life enhancing. Especially if it's been raining, the air feels clean and fresh and new; pine woods and there's always one of them not to far away are so invigorating that we try to bottle the smell of them and take it home with us.

And similar to woodland are orchards, apple orchards are a favourite.

If you live near the sea, then that oceanic saltiness is pervading, how often have you noticed that you can smell the sea long before you can actually see it, and that's another smell we try to take home with us. We had a Labrador once, who was really well trained, but take her anywhere she could smell the sea and she would head off full of the joys of youth and tear headlong straight into the water like the puppy she always was in her head. Smells can do that to us possibly like no other sense can.

They also stay in our memories longer maybe than any other sense. As a child I used to go and stay with my Grandmother for long periods, and one of my oldest memories was walking past the coffee shop which I think was in Mercery Lane. It had coffee beans in the window, and they ground coffee in there to order, sometimes my Gran would buy some. I hated it. Sorry to say, coffee, to me then, as now, is a very unpleasant aroma, but the memory has always been there and when my wife is making coffee, what she calls, 'real' coffee anyway I am transported back to that five-year-old in Mercery Lane walking passed, or even worse, into that shop.

Food aromas are particularly powerful, especially the implied flavours that we will later taste, or in some cases avoid. Sometimes they enhance the prospect of eating although they add nothing to it, the smell of garlic when cooking roast potatoes is mouth-watering, but actually adds little to the eating. In fact, the smell of food actually makes us feel hungry. We want to eat the product so much.

Given the opportunity where do we want to eat so much, well, outside obviously and we have many justifications for it too. Bar-be-ques are a very popular pastime, or eating alfresco, we love to sit outside at a café if we can. Or go for a picnic. And often in the winter too. For many years at home a New Year's BBQ was an essential tradition. We will often say how much better food tastes when we're outside. Even when out on a winters walk and we stop for lunch, food tastes just a little better.

Funny though how with so many things in our lives, the natural version always has the edge in being best...

3. Sight

The thing that lets us see. I think that it is important to make a distinction here, obviously we all see, well, unless we are blind, but even that needs a distinction. And I do not mean grades, you see there is a huge difference, or gulf between seeing and actually looking, and if you look but don't see then are you as blind as someone who has lost their sight. So maybe there are three levels of sight.

First if biologically, you have lost your sight that is obviously a tragedy, although there is a possible payoff which we will discuss later. Second, everyone else can see, but how many actually look. Which is the third level, actually seeing the detail in front of you.

Confused, well here is an example. You walk across a field, following a footpath and at the end of the footpath there is a wood. I know people who will never see passed that reality, well unless it's been raining and then, assuming they allowed themselves to even get that far, all they would see is the fact that it's muddy and maybe slippery too.

However, if you go one step further and really look, you will see a whole different world. Yes, acknowledging the conditions is important, if you don't you will end up on your bottom and that would be no fun, sore, dirty and quite possibly wet. But look further, what's on the horizon? What's across the field and what's right next to you? The horizon may even change its proximity depending on where you are and how your movements adjust the way you see your surroundings. On top of a clear hill the horizon maybe miles away and in a woodland very close. It might even be that woodland. If there is nothing obviously close to you, maybe a ploughed and disced field then you might be looking for movement that would indicate a bird, or rabbit, or insect, or..... The potential list is endless. For me, my focus is usually on birds, or insects, but I'm curious about anything. Buzzards are fairly common where we live and they are big, majestic birds that give me sense that all is right with the world, after all as top predators, if the ecology on the ground is wrong, they are the first to go. Watch the big female, with clearly noticeable fingers on her wings over 1m in span. Brown and white and all the shades in between, as she glides across our skies, wings in a flat glide. Awesome, a buzzard day will be a good day.

And woodland. Goes without saying, but have you ever really looked at the bark of a tree? A pine for instance, when you first see it, the bark looks deeply cracked almost as a landscape that has been parched and cracked at random as the ground drained of water. It could be a dried up river bed. Maybe with a strand of ivy thickening as it makes its way skyward up the trunk. As you consciously move in closer, you begin to notice the darker colours of the 'cracks' that are present all the way up the trunk, they make their way up the trunk almost randomly, it's then that you begin to notice that the 'islands' between the cracks are almost scalloped in their terrain, it almost looks like a woodsman has set about the surface with a hammer and chisel, carving out lines much like the sea often does to sand as it rises and falls up a beach. Without getting in close and really looking you will miss so much.

Touching the barks of different trees you begin to notice just how different they all are. A Yew or pine have a bark that is almost warm to the touch, almost fluffy, but compare that to the comparatively smooth hardness of a sycamore or Ash which is cold to the touch and the difference is clear. And if you are really brave you could touch a hawthorn, but remember it's got the word thorn in it for a reason. You don't have to be a tree 'hugger', not that there is anything wrong in that, just a tree 'toucher'. Just revel in the fact that in an ancient woodland many of the trees are just that, ancient, and if you stop for a moment, if you feel nothing else just let that sense of wonder wash over you.

So, back to buzzards, buzzards are resident all year round and very visible in their habits, but if it's summer you might see a dragonfly or damselfly and these insects are just to most about the most visually stunning creatures on this planet. Beginning their existence when dinosaurs roamed the earth, they are a very successful insects of the order Odonata. Visually they are unbelievable in the colours they demonstrate, the red of a Red Darter, unmissable as they dart passed you, the blue of a common damselfly and the green of an emperor dragonfly, almost 10cm across the wings or from head to tail. Or the black wing spots on a banded demoiselle, which I reckon set about the stories of fairies, unless of course fairies are real!

The colours are all just superb, eye catchingly awesome with an iridescence that should never be missed, for me can't be missed. It's that looking and seeing thing again. Probably there are only a few rivals from any other species they could be the kingfisher, that blue is superb, or the mallard and the magpie. Unless of course you leave the country.

But you've got to actually look, it wasn't that long ago, at Kearsney Abbey that I watched a kingfisher fly the whole length of the lake in full daylight, in front of several hundreds of picnickers, or dog walkers, or walkers or café goers and I am pretty sure I was the only person to see it.

Other birds that have stunning colours to look out for are male mallard, splashing about in our rivers and streams. The male has the most stunning, almost emerald green head that has an amazing almost luminescent feel to it as the winter or spring sun reflects of it. Superb. Or the shimmering metallic blue that you just catch as a magpie flies away at the last minute reluctant to leave whatever it is scavenging, but again as its back catches the sun that blue flickers as its motion changes the angles and rays of the sun.

Winter and spring are the best time of year to look at birds, they have finished their moult and are preparing for the breeding season so look their very best, ready to attract a mate, before all that courtship and then business of feeding youngsters after which they will be exhausted and tired and look it because as any parent knows, kids are hard work.

Ducks go a stage further than most birds and loose virtually all distinguishing marks during late summer in what we call eclipse colouring, so the challenge then is on to even recognise a bird as a mallard never mind look for the green head of a male.

Anyway, back to that walk. Many birds use posts as vantage points and will take off as you approach or stay in the hedgerows and call in alarm as you approach, but that is part of another chapter. You might though see the movements of flocks of birds as they use the hedgerow as a roadway, giving food and shelter as well as a safe way to travel. And what is in that hedgerow? In this fair Isle the number of plants is not only of interest in itself, it can also act as a guide to the age of the hedgerow. The number of species (not including annual growers like stinging nettles) minus one represents the number of hundred years it's likely to have been there. On our local estate there is one hedge that has been calculated to have been there since Saxon times. Anyway, I digress, again, using our power of sight to actually look we will probably see species like, elder, blackthorn, hawthorn, rose, dog-rose, ash, hazel amongst many others and ivy working its way up through the others and stinging nettles or cow parsley or hogweed growing around the base of the hedge.

You might also see the colours change as do the seasons, in woodland, the anemones painting the floor white in March before giving way to bluebells in April or May who in turn give way to shade loving plants like Ivy, successful everywhere or garlic when the trees grow leaves, and their canopies take hold.

Then in our garden's honesty shows reddy purple before lavenders and hebes become blue or pink, fuchsias begin their long reign and salvias change from white to red and both in between. As summer builds so buddleias and lafaterias stand tall and proud and show their huge flowering communities that butterflies and bumbles love so much. Peacock butterflies cover them in summer months. Foxgloves and roses make their appearances, foxgloves every other year, but it's a joy to watch the flowers as they descend the stem, and hollyhocks, the single version mind, often so tall they need help to stay vertical.

As we move into winter, the viburnham with its slightly reddish white flowers and mahonia, one of the 'nasty viscous bastard plants' with its spiky leaves giving us that glorious yellow spread of flowers so bold against that drab green we often get in winter before the first sign of snowdrops in late winter. Or camelias, with those magnificent large pink flowers can brighten up any landscape and will often flower all winter.

Even the aforementioned hedgerows will tell you the time of year, Hawthorn and black thorn or elder showing their blossom in spring, often reaching into early summer. Often hawthorn will paint a whole hedgerow white in spring, their flowers giving way to fruit in the autumn, when the same hedgerow will gain an almost reddish hue. And in September when we go and harvest sloes, the fruit of the black thorn to make gin which we look forward to drinking at Christmas.

And looking, we also see movement, obvious really, but often it's the movement that makes us look and take pleasure from what we see. A classic example is putting out food for birds, sparrows are often the most entertaining recipients. Food is not as readily available for them in our fields as once it was. So seed in a feeder is a welcome bonus. Especially for a bird species that has family politics in evidence as females dislodge the youngsters and males dislodge everybody, even displaying their own 'pecking' order. Watching a flock of 20 or so birds is so entertaining. It's all that movement that catches our attention.

For so many of us, it's not until someone points out the beauty that surrounds us that we actually see it.

Have you ever watched hoverflies in summer? They'd like us to think they are wasps, but the similarity stops at the black and yellow of their abdomen. Harmless in behaviour and abilities, but fairly easily distinguished from the more venomous insects they try to emulate, probably as a form of protection. You just have to look.

Hoverflies are flies, so there for only have two wings as opposed to the four of a wasp. They don't have the skinny waist of a wasp. And as their name suggests they hover, a lot. In fact they hover so much that is how they got their name, hovering in one spot and then flying to the next and hovering there for a while. Why? No idea, but they must have and they must like it, or see some advantage to it because they do it all the time. Wasps can hover too, but you'll never really see them do it like a hover fly. And for the gardeners, the larvae gobble up aphids so we should encourage them all we can. Just watch them, use the sight you have because they are one of the joys of our summer. And incidentally they don't have any fascination for our sweet picnic foods, another point in their favour. With a hoverfly you can enjoy your cream tea in peace.

So, to finish, a little science. Light goes into our eyes and is received by rods and cones at the back of the eye, well after the pupil has adjusted its size so that the amount of light we receive is safe and won't blind us, then focussed by the lens before falling on the rods and cones at the back of the eye. They then convert the information contained into electromagnetic signals that our brain decodes. The rods are mostly used at night and only deal with black, white and grey light, whilst the cones are mostly operable in daylight and handle the colour part of vision. Which is why moths for example are virtually all grey and butterflies are very colourful. There is no point in being colourful if no one can see your splendours. I know that's not entirely true, but it's a large part of why, and it's nice to think that it's just for us.

Incidentally, light goes into the eye and not the other way around. A common misconception amongst children, and as I'm increasingly finding, adults too. If light came from our eyes we would walk about as if we had two torches on our face.

4. Sound

And so we come to sound. So often, when I look around at the people I share this world with so many are lost in their own little world and the most obvious strategy is put other sounds into our ears. And it's easy to see (!) because people with headphones or ear pods are everywhere. People are often walking around watching videos, aware of nothing around them, wishing to be anywhere except where they are, or talking to other people, or listening to music. And surely all these things, distractions, should be a part of our lives, just not the whole of it.

Whilst at work yesterday a robin was singing, as I write this it's January, it had just changed its song. The robin has a marvellous song that has so many messages that dramatically change for spring. As one of the few birds that sing boldly all year round, they sonically brighten up our 'silent' summers. The reason for this is that they are very territorial, and their song is a warning for any other robin, a veritable warning no less. Both sexes sing for that very reason. Normally they are telling all that this is their patch and everything on it is theirs too, all trees, areas of grass, food, plants, perches, worms, maggots or any other item of importance to a robin. Hence both sexes need to sing, it's just that in spring that this has to change, or we'd have no more robins, they change their song, all the above is still true, but with one exception, if you're of the opposite sex and want to come in and make babies then you're welcome. Well at least until the youngsters fledge and then its back to rule one, and they go back to their regular song.

Which is also why if you see a robin without a red breast it's a juvenile, not a female. The adults look alike, only distinguishable by robins themselves, which is handy. If the youngsters had red breasts the adults would attack them as invading birds. And robins will fight to the death if they see the need, real warriors of the bird world.

It was whilst enjoying the stark cutting song of a robin, beautiful on a fresh winters day that I was somewhat dismayed when my son connected his speaker to his phone and played some extremely good rock music whilst we were working. Music that at a more sensitively chosen time I would appreciate.

But sounds are everywhere and often the best context for listening is that of right where we are. I am not a great fan of any urban environment, but I can clearly remember staying in a hotel in London and leaving the window open purely so that I could hear the traffic noise, with the occasional siren of emergency vehicles, or the hooters of those impatiently pushing and shoving. I wouldn't want these sounds anywhere else, but there it was entirely fitting. Incidentally, I was staying in London because I had been to see a rock gig, I think it had been Dragonforce, very loud and noisy. In a concert venue, in a city, entirely appropriate. Music festivals in the countryside are also just as awesome, as long as it's the occasional event. The point I am trying to make is that city sounds are entirely appropriate in a city and country sounds are entirely appropriate in the country, it is when we use sounds out of context on a regular basis that can be disappointing or annoying. Or the way that many people use sound to isolate themselves from their environment.

Hence my displeasure at the rock music over the robin. It can be difficult not to preach on these occasions...

But, there's always a but, can you imagine any countryside with no sound? I remember watching a documentary with Tony Soper (remember him) and he made that same statement and then they turned off the mike. Silence! So wrong. Just think in a woodland there are so many sounds almost all the time, wind in the trees, branches and twigs banging into each other, rustlings on the ground as lots of different creatures do their thing. Rarely is there not a bird singing, tits chattering, robins as mentioned above, a wren or blackbird alarm calling, probably because of you. And in our busy world there are usually manmade sounds in the background.

Even in our busy towns and cities there are quiet havens, parks and gardens, but often some of the best places for peace and quiet are canals and rivers. Often they're below the level of the bustling cities above, or the roads are in the distance. Regents Canal in London or the Tiber in Rome are classic examples, just descending down to them you can 'hear' the city 'noise' recede into the distance and all of a sudden, we can hear again. Again, usually the sounds of birds are what we hear first, or even the gentle throb of a diesel engine as a boat or barge chugs passed.

But often the best thing about our sense of hearing is the ability to hear silence, leaving the sound of everyday life behind, or at the least recede into the distance. And when we do this the ability to think increases as the unconscious part of our brain can emerge through the cacophony of sound we surround ourselves with. How often has a thought just popped into your mind unexpectedly at these moments? I had one the other day, obvious really, stop trying to figure out how to get those who won't listen to listen. I have often said, 'those who need us the most want us the least'. No point, they will not listen, concentrate on those who will, maybe they'll sort out those who won't.

And if we then add those gentle and soothing sounds that put us further at ease, we can really let our imaginations fly. The sound of water running, or falling gently into a pool, wind when it blows gently can make leaves or bamboo stems for example take on a life of their own. When the song of a blackbird, of the repeating call of a songthrush cuts through the silence the change can be dramatic. Even noticing the change of direction or force of the wind will put a smile on your face.

Ultimately, it's giving yourself the opportunity and time to engage with the world around you and sound is possibly the strongest connection we can have with the world around us, especially if we temporarily stop looking.

So often we can identify the creatures around us more by the sounds they make than by actually seeing them. Especially in the case of bird song, and some of them are easy, as I said above the thrush, if the bird is repeating everything it sings, two, three, four or more times it's a song thrush. If it's very loud, and a littler harsh (comparatively) it's a robin, more melodic and probably a wren, which can also be distinguished by its 'ticking' warning call, wren scolding as the cliché goes. If it sounds like a seventies car horn then it's a chaffinch. Did you ever read Beatrix Potter, 'a little bit of bread and no cheese', then you have a yellowhammer the specs for ID are endless.

Funny how the sound of silence is far from silent, if you just listen.

And as ever, a little science. Sound is funnelled into the ears. The bigger the earlobe, the more you hear. Elephants must hear very well. And certainly, the big dishes that can be found on the Kent coast from time to time are there and huge to catch sounds, echoes, coming from out to sea. The sound then makes the ear drum vibrate which passes to the ossicles which then passes vibrations through the fluid in the cochlea which causes hairs to bend which sends signals to the brain.

Have you noticed we have all these receptors which use different methods of converting all those things that we sense into electric signals. Our brains exist by sending and receiving electric signals. Which is a really significant part of our connection to the world we live in. Concentrate now!!!

So, we come to taste.

5. Taste

Now when you think about it, everything (almost?!?) we taste comes from the great outdoors. The only reason I qualify it, is that you can never be sure these days, but as all growth initiates from the sun, it goes kind of hand in hand. All plants use heat from the sun to drive their systems, photosynthesis converts light energy into chemical energy which drives all their systems. They take in carbon dioxide that we breathe out and convert it to the oxygen we need to breathe. Plants are eaten by herbivores which turn the plants they eat into energy for their systems, and they in turn are eaten by carnivores which turn them into energy for their systems.

What's a system you ask? Well, all the parts of anything that work together to make the thing work. And the 'thing' we are talking about here is any organism on this planet. The thing, or organism that is the subject of this text ultimately, is us.

And boy, do we like to taste. Especially if we want to meet people, whether on a date, or to discuss business, or even just for the pleasure of it. It's the one sense that has businesses created all around it, café's, restaurants, and public houses to name a few. And the range of flavours and cuisines is almost endless. Add a few smells and the result is intoxicating.

Taste is so socially enshrined in our societies we create it to impress, give a social occasion an extra dose of importance. We ask people round to taste various different foods, and of course beers and wines, each with their own subtle band of flavours. There are also clubs based on just these desires. We even travel to other outsides around the world for further variety.

But do you know where most people will tell you food tastes best? Well, outside of course, why do you think we go on so many picnics and have so many bar-b-ques? It's because it does, all our senses are enlivened outside. It is where we came from. We'll also eat out on the veranda where possible for the same reason.

When we got out there and there's food to eat, we eat it, because it's as fresh as it can get and as we know, the fresher the better, that's why we go to such lengths to keep it as fresh as possible, or find ways to preserve it. Who hasn't walked passed brambles in autumn and not enjoyed, or occasionally exclaimed at the sharpness of, a blackberry?

Foraging has become quite a buzz word these days. That is because there's so much out there we can eat, but we have lost the knowledge of what we can eat, or not eat. You wouldn't eat just any mushroom for instance, because some of them are just not good for you. But those that are, delicious. And the number of things that can be made into a drink, tea for example, in this country camomile, is almost endless.

Why is food so important for so many occasions, especially when we meet new people? Well, because it opens up conversations. How often have been out with someone, especially someone we want to impress, whether you are on a date, or a prospective new business partner, and conversation starts to dry up only for it to kick in with renewed vigour when the food arrives, it's a kind of conversation lubricant. One might even ponder as to how the world ever made any kind of social or political progress without the sharing of food.

One on it's own? Not really...

In truth, and you've probably noticed whilst reading this text, it's virtually impossible to treat any of the senses in isolation. It's really hard when talking about birdsong for example not to talk the bird and how it looks, everything about a bird goes together, it's appearance, it's shape, the sound of its song or the alarm calls it makes. How it moves and the way it's form has developed to allow it to be successful in making a living. The fact that often you will hear it before you see it.

Or the smell of honeysuckle, or jasmine, or as the cliché says, 'smell the roses'. On a calm day, or evening we smell the scent before we see the flower.

In fact, often the sense of hearing or smell actually directs our eye to the source before we see it. Almost as if they were designed to be detectors for our eyes, in fact often other senses heighten our expectation of what we are about to see before the object comes into view.

Could you imagine going into any environment, the outside especially, where you could only experience it through limited senses. A countryside with no sounds, no wind whether howling or whispering, the clashing of trees trunks or the brushing of bamboo, birdsong, sweet and lilting like the wren or harsh shrieks of a barn owl. Smells like the damp smell of life-giving earth we lift to our noses to enhance, which also contains decaying matter of varying forms, leaves, insects and of course poo. We pick it up and smell it, and of course that brings in touch too.

Even our cities and towns have their aromas, and sounds, all of which inform our vision. The smell of exhaust fumes, or wastes, often overpowering the pleasant smells, and the noise of traffic that drowns the sound of birdsong made by birds that never stop valiantly calling, the drive to find a mate that never goes away.

And as I mentioned before: the touch and taste of the air as it passes into our lungs, fresh and refreshing, revitalising. We can almost feel it pass to every part of our body, from the top of our head to the extremities of our fingers and toes.

Our sense of smell will predict what the food that comes to our plate will look like, which is why chefs will go to such great lengths to make sure our food looks as good on arrival to our eyes as predicted by our noses and then our taste buds. We don't like to eat something that looks, or for that matter smells horrible.

In fact, we almost need all three senses to actually identify the food put in front of us, there have been game shows where people tasted food blindfold and couldn't work out what they were eating, but I guess that was the point. Can you imagine the confusion if you mixed up the smell of one type of food with that of another?

In truth, we take everything for granted, work, money, food and drink and the people we share our lives with, just as much as the senses we use to experience the world in which we live. It's not until any one or maybe even several of the 'things' we take for granted are taken from us do we actually understand or value their worth.

Funny then, that with the loss of 'sight' the other senses actually seem to get heightened as if understanding the real value of their worth. And if you actually doubted that fact, take a few moments and sit down somewhere you will be undisturbed for a while, outside preferably. Ten minutes should do it, close your eyes and just 'sit'. Very soon you will realise you are hearing things almost louder than you ever did before and you will begin to judge the distances of the things you can hear as you possibly never have and pay attention to the direction the sounds are coming from. You will smell the world more than you ever did. The flower you were never aware of, who is having a bar-be-que or the exhaust of next doors car. You will become more aware of what you are sitting on and what you are touching with your hands, you will be more aware of the temperature of the air and of what you are sitting on. Even if it is damp.

But if you then open your eyes, you may see something you have never seen before, birds will come close by if you are still, especially robins and blackbirds, or hoverflies, which will stay hello and then buzz off before hovering in their next spot. Dragonflies will land on you, freezing you on the spot as you try to prolong their stay. On a recent walk we had participants watching foxes just metes away and kestrels hunting just overhead. Wildlife often needs just a little stillness to come close whether just to say hello or sing loudly. And close proximity from a wild soul is an honour that should always be celebrated.

So temporarily suspending our sense of sight allows our other senses to be heightened which is surely a triumph in itself, but also allows us to see our world in greater definition due to a closeness we don't or can't experience without actually making a conscious decision to do so. But ultimately, it's all about making intentional decisions with ourselves and our senses and where we put ourselves to enhance the quality of the lives we lead.

Isn't it?

The rest of the world

Whilst that's how the senses feel to us as humans in how we use, abuse or block them, it's worth remembering that all animals have evolved to suit different habitats, eat and hunt different foods in different habitats and at different times of day. We spend most of our time using our senses of sight and sound predominantly. We are awake primarily during the day and use our sense of sound to help us react appropriately to danger, relax and communicate. Smell, taste, and touch unconsciously for the most part. Well, unless we have trained ourselves to behave differently.

Many of the animals we share our world with have evolved differently and have senses balanced very differently, often with a different sense taking priority. An eagle can see movement eight times further away than we can and thus can see the movement of a rabbit up to two miles away. An owl can see far better than we can at night in the dark. The balance between rods and cones is very different to our, they have many more rods, so although they see very little colour, (less need for it at night), they pick up a lot more light. But they cannot see in total dark any more than we can. Their ears are also at different heights, very handy, not only can they tell left and right from sounds made around them, but they can also detect up and down. If they hear a sound they can move their head so that they are looking straight at the location of whatever made the sound. If you have ever watched a great grey owl hunt rodents, it's a visual treat. From a roosting position in a tree they will just descend to the snow covered ground and impact right at the point that their prey made the noise, often with great success. An amazing skill to be able to hunt your dinner when you can't even see it.

Spiders use their sense of touch to detect vibrations in a web, bats use sound to find their way about and to both catch food and to avoid becoming anything else's dinner.

Mans best friend uses their sense of smell first most of the time. If you watch a dog, especially when out and on the loose, they are continually sniffing. A dog's world is full of aromas, and they tend to have a fascination for the more unsavoury ones in my experience, every scent marking, and poo deposit must be investigated. It also one of the reasons we domesticated them, and I dare say, they allowed themselves to be domesticated. It's a great trade off. Skills for food. We use them to track people, items, and other prey on a regular basis, as well as to herd animals and provide protection or early warning system. They also have great hearing. How often have you thought your dog was barking 'for no reason'. They always have a reason, it's just that we can't hear it. That is why we use them as guard dogs in the first place. We should trust them more.

And what about number 6?

Of course, we all like to think we have a sixth sense, or GUT feeling. The cliché 'trust your gut' didn't come from nowhere, and we all like to think we know what it means, or what it is. But what is it? And where does it come from? And is it really even a sense at all?

Not really extra sensory perception, although that might be handy. Just something based on intuition, a feeling, or just something we can't explain.

How often have you 'felt' something is just not right or is just too good to be true. You are offered an amazing deal on a product... The cliché, if something is too good to be true, then it probably is...

Or the reverse, you turn down an amazing and genuine offer, because you refuse to believe it...

Or that there is someone behind you, although there is no physical, or sensory reason for knowing so, and then had someone appear.

Or coincidence, so called, when someone, who you haven't seen for ages, pops into your mind and you see them the next day. Even more bizarrely you meet them when you are on holiday.

Or thankfully rarely, for no reason whilst driving along a road, you turn off or stop for no apparent reason and seconds later a car going too fast goes down the road you were just on.

How often do things happen that seemed absolutely awful at the time? You didn't get the dead cert job, only to discover your likely employer was about to go out of business, and because you didn't get that job, you still have one.

Bizarrely, you might say, even the outdoors can pull on that sixth sense. I have had occasions where I have had a 'real' pull to be outdoors, might just have been a dose of claustrophobia, but it has felt much more like a pull to me, and when I have got outside I have seen a spectacular natural phenomenon.

It is then up to the individual to place meaning onto these events, whether accepting them for just what they are or whether to ascribe a deeper significance.

The word of caution though, be careful you don't mistake 'gut' feeling for emotional decision making, because that will almost always lead to disaster. Business decisions must be based on reason and not emotion, but that is not a topic for this text. If you still want something a week later then its probably not an emotional decision... And if you don't think sixth sense should be here, that's fine too.

In Summary

Put simply then. Stop, look, near, far, what's moving, what colour is it; listen, birdsong, the buzzing of insects, the wind in the trees, the sound of traffic (hopefully in the distance); touch (you don't have to hug trees, but go on, touch them), the earth, grass, whatever; and when you've picked it up smell it, along with the scents of plants, the air and if possible taste the fruits (and if you know enough, the leaves or edible fungi) that surround us.

Give yourself time to do all these things, take some of them indoors and continue to appreciate them. Just remember insects need the plants to keep us alive, so don't take very many.

Now one last point to make. I have referred to most of the senses and how they are all connected to our brains by electricity, electrical impulses. Energy... We run on these signals. Now we also know that our Earths core is full of electromagnetic fields, and so is our solar system. Which means we actually do have a direct connection to the outside world, what happens in the earth and our solar system has a direct connection to us and affects the way we behave and the way we think. It cannot be any other way. The fact that some days we are happy or sad, for no reason we can ascertain. And whilst we are on that subject, we also know we are 70% water, and we know what the moon does to the oceans. It is where the term lunatic comes from. And if you look at the cycles of the moon and note down how you feel you are likely to notice a pattern with your emotions, or headaches or whatever. And some of us are far more effected than others. With the moon it all comes down to gravity and energy.

Energy, because, as you know, the sun is where the light and heat energy that is at the beginning of all food chains, and therefore life chains as well, comes from. Light can be reflected, is reflected, all the time. Just look in a mirror. The light we see coming from the moon is reflected light. The moon does not emit light like the sun, or a torch for that matter, it is all reflected from the sun. Light is energy, so on a night with a 'full' moon, more energy is transmitted to the Earth, which affects all people to varying degrees. The full moons in March, April and May, often called supermoons are much closer to us on Earth and therefore have an even greater effect on those that have a greater receptiveness to energy, because the energy has a shorter distance to travel and is therefore stronger.

As a result, it makes sense to try to acknowledge and understand, just a little, the connection we have...

Just maybe there is something out there bigger than us, just maybe...

Edge

Eyes look bright

Furtive at night

A movement, making leaves rustle

Wind makes flames flicker

A cloak drops all caffufle

A heart beats a little quicker

Wings beat slowly passed a moon bright

Eyes still, in a head that scans movement on the edge of sight

Chapter Six.

An Unexpected Moment 1.

Someone said that life is like a highway. They were right, there's loads of lanes and left and right turns, and each change of direction will have a different outcome. We often have a pre-planned destination, however, we can change our mind at any time. But sometimes we change our minds with little notice for any number of reasons and what follows is sometimes random, sometimes unexpected and of varying scales.

So, this little gem was the result of a change of mind.

Returning from our current work site earlier than planned because I just had so much to do in the office, I was driving along the straight above Sutton. As I approached the left-hand turn and dropped down forge hill I noticed a kestrel shaped object in a tree, sitting on a branch over hanging the road. As I got closer it alighted from the tree and descended towards the road levelling off at maybe 30 or 40 cm's above the road and glided for several yards before flapping generally four times to gain a little bit of height before gliding once more.

Not a kestrel then, they don't fly like this.

It continued to fly like this for most of the descent down the hill. I glanced at the speedo in my car, it was keeping up a steady 30 mph, using gravity obviously, but also pretty streamlined. Just as we were nearing the entrance to Winkland Oaks Cottages it went straight up into the air and over the hedge and was gone.

By now I had already identified the bird by it colours, size and style of flight, but if I had any remaining doubts, this behaviour clinched it. Sparrowhawk. A female sparrowhawk at that.

So, firstly, it's style of flight, sparrowhawks can be identified by their flight pattern, flap flap, flap flap glide. It's pretty species specific and is useful for distinguishing them, at a distance from pigeons, that fly either in straight lines, or have a very exaggerated undulating flight. And whilst male sparrowhawks are similar in size to a kestrel, albeit bluer, the females are very brown and typically for all raptors much larger. Not that I could tell from this distance, or speed though, but sparrowhawks are very barred, all the way across the chest and down to the tails, spreading across the wings too. But the superpower of the sparrowhawk is the way it generally surprises its prey and that is to kind of flip over a hedge at speed and catch any unsuspecting smaller bird on the other side before it's had a chance to make a run for it. Often funnily enough, a sparrow... But they can take anything up the size of a partridge, making them very popular with game keepers, but that's a whole other story.

Why so special? Well sparrowhawks are not uncommon, although possibly uncommonly seen, this behaviour when it occurs is over in a flash and unless your watching spot has the requisite habitat you will still not see this behaviour very often. We do see them occasionally on top of the hedge at home that the sparrows use as a hotel for shelter when feeding from the feeder, often mantling their catch as they eat it, or even more rarely try to give me a parting as they zoom from garden to garden again trying to catch the unsuspecting songbird., to actually track one as it lines up its attack and then flips over the hedge is just so utterly unreal. Probably only lasted 10 – 15 seconds at most, but a sight so special that life seemed to almost slow down, a breath holdingly awesome WOW moment. I also hold myself fortunate that I know enough to know what I was seeing and can appreciate it for what it was.

And I only saw it because I had to change plans and inadvertently put myself in a location where it would be possible to see such a wonderful sight, at the moment that it happened.

And even more strangely I passed my wife, just as I neared home, going the other way. When she got home, she reported seeing an unknown bird of prey. Nothings guaranteed, but you know what it probably was...

Funny that!

Chapter Seven.

The search for church (Part One).

Rome, or I guess to be more precise (in a general kind of way), Italy, has an exorbitantly large number of Cathedrals. But for me it was Rome where this began to become abundantly clear, firmly established when we reached Venice. I had never thought about it before. I had become 'sort of' spiritual through my use of meditation and growing sense of awareness of what was around me but had never really dwelt on the notion of churches, or in this context, cathedrals before.

Canterbury, and other cities obviously, had cathedrals and they were all magnificent buildings and I quite liked to go in, but that was about it. Churches were where you might go to get married or sing carols at Christmas, if you couldn't get out of it. Architecturally interesting, but mostly just part of the scenery.

My wife and I were on our honeymoon in Italy. We, or I guess mostly my wife, had planned a road trip, starting in Sorrento and working our way north via several tourist hotspots. Driven by my love of Roman history, and Ducati motorcycles and Gillian's desire to go to Florence and straighten up the leaning tower of Pisa. I think we both wanted to go to Venice, and we had to go to Lake Como because that was where Senator Amidalas palace was filmed (Star Wars). Obviously.

We arrived in Rome by train and went for a mystery tour of 'hotspots' by taxi, before we were dropped at our hotel. We had wondered why our taxi driver had been less than pleased with his fare when we got in. Our hotel, as we found out when we walked it departing Rome, was only a ten-minute walk from the train station, took over half an hour by taxi!

The first activity we had booked was a bus ride around the capitol. We had had to rush to get to the departure point on time and were less than impressed to find that it was actually a 'walking bus'. I already had blisters on the back of my ankles, can't remember why, I also only had deck shoes on, not that good for walking, especially when you have said, blister on your foot. After a great deal of consternation and discussion of all the various options and, it has to be said the constructive sympathy of the tour guide, we worked out a solution so inspired and unacceptable to any but those truly in love, that it had to be considered genius. My wifes need for her blister plasters and socks was far less than mine and so she lovingly gifted me her used blister plaster and the trip, much less the day, was saved.

We had signed up for this trip to give ourselves some idea of where things were and what we might like to investigate further, and in that it was a great success, not that we realised why at the time. Plenty of buildings were pointed out and their significance discussed, we visited the Roman Pantheon and the Atrevi falls, we had some ice cream at a gelatino, of great significance, but information was coming at us thick and fast and we were just soaking up the vibe, so, so much was lost on us, but the ice cream, or gelato, as we should call it was to die for and I should add here that gelato for lunch has become a staple of many holiday lunches, especially during our honeymoon.

The tour finished at the Spanish Steps, and whilst they are magnificent in themselves, we returned there two days later, principally to visit the Keats House and museum. An unexpected bonus when you have an interest in all things Gothic and Pre Raphaelite, along with any other associate.... sad really, with all that on his doorstep, Keats saw virtually nothing of Rome dying in his rooms of consumption.

Having returned to the sunshine of a springtime Rome after the gloom of Keats' place we decided to ascend the Spanish Steps, climbing all 138 of them from the Piazza di Spagna to the heights of the Piazza Trinita dei Monti where we stood, shall we say perspiring, and admiring the view across the rooftops of Rome. Being English and coming from a country where the sun is only just beginning to warm up the air, the heat of Italy and the exertion of an uphill climb required us to acclimatise once again and the view provided all motivation required.

As we found temperature neutral my wife suggested we should have a look inside the Franciscan Church of Santissima Trinita dei Monti that had dominated the skyline as we had ascended, with it's beautiful twin towers

The church stands behind a monolith, and as is so common, ugly word, is rendered white, there are two cross shaped windows either side of the entrance which has a Roman Empire styled porch way, then another level above these with a half-circled window, a clock to the left and some ornate carvings to the right before the two towers make their ascent into the sky.

Boldly walking in, Gillian rounds and we leave, somewhat puzzled I follow. Gillian is wearing shorts and has her shoulders exposed, she can't go in. I have a t shirt and my shorts are hardly short, well how many self-respecting rock fans wear short shorts anymore? So I am instructed to go in and experience it for both of us. Still slightly bemused I then re-enter and have a look around.

And to me it's a 'church'. There's a lot of them about, great vibe and all that, but all I'm really interested in is outside. So after a brief look around, I leave and re-enter the cities heat and go to find my wife.

Even the Vatican didn't do it for me. Don't get me wrong, it's a magnificent city, but very austere and far too full of its own self-importance. I can even accept that I had to wear trousers in that heat, but the way you are directed through its halls and corridors and porticos, and the like is, well, for me anyway, just too much. There comes a point when you have seen so many wonderful paintings, or tapestries, or busts, or statues that they all just start to look the same and any significance is lost. By the time we got to the Sistine Chapel I had lost interest completely. It doesn't even have a feeling of church to it. It's just a big box room covered in the most amazing artwork, which is totally jaw droppingly awesome, or it would be if you weren't suffering overkill already, with the paraphernalia required for services by the Pope et al. It's not that I don't understand the significance, I know how important the place is, it just wasn't special to me, at least not that day anyway.

St. Peters Square on the other hand is just so awesome. And I mean really awesome, in the way it doesn't even have to try to be, it just is. It's huge, as in really mega big huge. The circular lay out and all the lines leading to or from the obelisk, the columned walkways that surround the 'circular' square. The statues that overlook all who visit for whatever purpose. The 'street' that leads up to it, it's all just almost surreal, as are the size of the crowds, we would have liked to go into St. Peters Basilica, another name for Cathedral that goes back to empire times, but not with queues that big. Time to go and look for a gelato.

So, the Vatican did not kick start my search for church either.

My journey, or search, to find church had unconsciously begun. We did visit a couple more in Rome, but the next major milestone in this inevitable part of my journey would take place in Venice, well after a rushed visit in Pisa.

The trip was rushed because I didn't pay enough for parking and hadn't realised how far away the tower was from where we parked or how much there was to see when we got there. I was popular, not! We had a very quick spin around the inside of the cathedral after we had eventually found the way in, and the story might have ended there but for the spectacular view of the roofs you get from the top of the tower.

The cathedral could have come straight from Lord of the Rings, or should that be the other way round, but you can imagine finding it in Osgiliath. Wonderful white walls, broken by horizontal strips of render, arches and windows. The roofs are all at traditional angles, flat with a series of small pillars at the apexes. There is a very scary looking set of steps on the right-hand side, all dominated by the magnificent dome which sits above a simple but ornate columned parapet, an almost middle eastern ball sits atop of that. With the exception of the dome and the round rear of the cathedral it is all a mass of straight lines and angles, all I'm sure designed to make sure you are aware of where some might say your place is in the world.

We descended from the tower and rushed out of the tower complex and headed back toward the car, this time we went through the town and considering we had been told there's nothing much to Pisa apart from the tower complex, we liked the town and definitely intend to return one day. The town deserves exploration and the complex itself should be taken at a much more leisurely pace.

Living there if you don't like gardening could be a bind though, everyone can see into your garden. We did get the necessary photo of my wife pushing the tower back straight though.

Still no great insights into my search for church though.

Eventually our minibus bus rolled into Venice, or at least the outskirts of it. Yes, I did say minibus. We had asked the vehicle hire company for an automatic. My wife figured it was one thing less to worry about driving on the 'other' side of the road in a foreign country. We were given a minibus big enough for twelve people. As you can imagine getting it out of the multistorey car park was just the first of our challenges with it. Going round a corner in one go was impossible, we had to do each one in two goes. We couldn't even get it into the carpark at one hotel.

Venice grows on you, slowly and inexorably with a relentlessness that cannot be ignored. Let me explain. We had arrived at midday, it was hot; on arrival at our hotel we quickly deposited our luggage and descended to the bar desperate for a cuppa. Our host told us not to be so stupid, pointed out the bus stop, told us which bus to get and ushered us out of the hotel. Must be an English thing, much as I admire her reasoning, all we really wanted at that moment was a cup of tea.

The bus arrived and dutifully we got on and found a seat. That was a good job too, we hadn't realised just how far out of the 'old', town we were. Twenty to twenty-five minutes out, and obviously that's both ways. We are deposited on the quay and cross a very large bridge into Venice central proper, we walk along the Grand Canal and are just awed by this amazing place. This is Venice and we are here, right now, and that's enough in itself.

You just can't help but be entranced, we all know what Venice looks like; no cars, well there are no roads, just the dominating canals, with boatmen all bustling and jostling to get to whatever their destination. Gondolas, and motorboats, for the haulage of both goods and people, of lots of differing sizes. You can buy a waterbus ticket to go wherever you wish. And the sounds of engines, hooters and people, cajoling, bartering, yelling for whatever purpose, or trying to sell you their wares, or food as you go is generally good natured, but in St. Mark's Square, very intrusive.

And then there are the buildings, huge houses with walls dominated by square or arched windows often several stories high, mostly white, or grey, but there are yellows and reds and oranges. Some look very sombre and European, but many with a great feel of the orient or other faraway places. As you explore you begin to find alley ways that are so easy to get lost in, shops that you can never find a second time. Signs that never seem to give directions regardless of the arrows that are abundant. You look up as well as left and right, the place is neck achingly beautiful.

All senses are assaulted, the smells of food, of crepes, breads and cakes, meals of pasta or pizza, all surrounded by the calls of the sellers or those sent out to find trade. Gondoliers looking to find fares for the next hour. Theatrical shops of great number, selling cloaks and masks of huge variety, size, colour and complexity. I imagine it must be hard to make a living here, overheads must be high and the competition is intense. There must be a time where even a place like Venice must sleep, and a season when tourism falls away.

There are squares or piazzas, loads of piazzas and they all have churches or cathedrals in them, and they are all so different, heights, shapes and sizes, even colour. On your first visit the whole place is bedazzling.

So, as I said, we crossed onto the path by the Grand canal and decided food was the most important thing and found a riverside restaurant and ordered a drink, and just let the reality of where we were sink in. We ordered what must be one of the most expensive meals we have ever eaten. It wasn't actually that good, there's always a dose of normality waiting to get you, but you have to let it pass right over you. As we did, obviously, and incidentally, we never did get a cup of tea.

We crossed over Ponte di Realto or the Rialto Bridge to us Brits and went exploring proper. By the time we returned to our hotel that evening we were knackered, and I can remember thinking, can I really do two more days of walking and exploring? Absolutely exhausted, my legs aching I fell asleep. However, by the time we did leave, as I said Venice had worked its magic on us and ingrained itself almost into our very souls.

The next day however, was where the search for church really kicked in.

The Church of Santa Maria Gloriosa dei Frari sits just off a canal path right in the centre of the loop the Grand Canal makes through Venice in the Campo dei Frari. Now it's a church, a huge church, so why is it not a cathedral, or a basilica (mentioned above)? Well, it's all to do with whether there's a bishop or similar, is doing a bit of admin or business there.

It's not that grand on the outside, in fact the main reason we went in was that Gillian had read somewhere that there was another tower in Venice to rival the one in St. Mark's Square and we thought this one might be it. The majority of the outside is brick work, although that does serve to make the ornamentation there really stand out, the arched doorway for example. Not Roman, but almost pointed at the top, with lots of ropework sculpted into it in many layers and stone columns on either side with statues atop of either, complimenting the one atop the arch itself. The columns barred at a meter a time, making them look a little grander even. The round windows surrounded by sculpture and colour that resemble the roulette wheels of a casino. Surely a coincidence...

The tower is to the rear and to the left of the church.

Anyway, in we went.

You can't actually go up the tower at all but that didn't matter, the vibe or atmosphere in the church was so much more 'churchy' than in many of those in the main city. And it was beautiful.

Almost Tardis like it was huge on the inside, there are four smaller churches on the inside, kind of like there are smaller shops in a shopping mall. The main church is separated from the rest by three magnificent, marbled walls all grey and silver and gold. Pictures two high separated by pillars, grey at the bottom, merging into silver and then gold, several sections expanding as they rise reaching to a section inscribed in latin, and on top, as is so typical, are various statues overlooking the scene, with regal arrogance. The main entrance to this most important of inner churches has a roman arch with the requisite Crucified Christ atop that.

Each corner is turreted before you see another wall mirrored on the one before. The altar is again ornate with crosses and regalia once again very grand with a magnificent scene painted on the walls behind. There is a lesser church and alter to either side; one the right there is the entrance to yet another church and alter, a little less grand this time.

Alongside this and church right is a piazza porticoed on all sides, the roof supported by grand pillars, the piazza itself holding statues and a font underneath the most grand of roofs supported by four pillars and atop of this angels and figures holding a cross most magnificent.

An interesting thought occurs, it is almost like a traditional castle layout. You enter the church through a grand entrance, a little like going through the outer defences of a castle with a drawbridge and grand gates, you then have the main communal area where the populace frequents and lives, i.e. the lesser churches and places of living and confession. The main keep, or in this case the grandest of alters is surrounded by another high wall and statues with turrets at the corners and an even greater entrance to further impress you and keep the prescribed version of your reality enforced.

The only place I have seen such sculpted figures this spectacular was Tyne Cot, the WW1 burial ground in Belgium. You have to wonder at the level of devotion it takes to build these places and wonder if it was with the blessing of the populace, or in spite of them. The Roman Catholic Church certainly likes to impress.

We explored every nook and cranny, the 4 separate chapels in it as well as the grand major one. After exploring, 'we sat down and had one of those deep and meaningful conversations that only happen at specific times and at specific places. Conversations that have a timeless level of honesty we rarely manage. We have these from time to time, usually unplanned, or there's no magic, to sort out anything that needs air, either current, or rising up from our pasts. We discovered later that we had sat for over one and a half hours. It really calmed us. We've had these chats before, but somehow in front of a cross, and in this church, gave this one an intensity greater than usual. Funny a church doing that!'

We visited several more churches after that, but none that had the same effect on us as The Church of Santa Maria Gloriosa dei Frari. Maybe there was something else at work on that visit. There were the ones that had the most fantastic purple on the pillars and walls, or reds or blues, all different and of a majesty both regal and inspiring.

It took us a little while to visit the church in Como, boringly called the Cathedral de Como, and again grand, but for us without the magic of De Frari. Incidentally, after the great number everywhere else Como only had the one. And somehow it was at its most magnificent in the view of it from our apartment window.

So, with all that had happened to me in the previous year or so, and with a book shortly to be released on the world, a sense of the worlds spirituality and my own, the significance of the buildings of religious dedication was becoming clear. On our return home I fully intended to spend a part of my time in churches. I think they are useful focus for the spirituality we can get from outdoors in general, or maybe a parallel stimulus, or even just an alternative place for calm, meditation and reflection. Anyhow, we know that change is as good as a rest in all things.

Funnily enough many churches are built upon sacred sites of many indigenous peoples by the conquering nations. I guess you can't 'flatten' spirituality...

Chapter eight.

Buzzard

Funnily enough, this book, once upon a time was going to be called 'A Buzzard Day is a Good Day'. Ultimately, I changed my mind because I don't think anyone else would have 'got it'. It also didn't really sum up what the book was about. What it did though was convey how much I am a fan of this beautiful and majestic bird.

Despite having a magnificent appearance and possibly holding great place in our world as the starting point for all other birds of prey, it has also demonstrated a magnificent ability to be resurgent and keep focus when all odds are down. The species is a survivor. They also offer a link, maybe perceived, to a resurgent way of thinking.

There is no doubt that when a buzzard is in the sky it's a good day and often there's a lesson to be learnt from them as you have/will read... I feel a connection, even to the point that if I haven't seen one for a while, I question why not.

So where did my journey to love buzzards begin? That is hard to say. They weren't my first love as raptors go, that's for sure. I love the way kestrel hovers, I love the stealth of sparrowhawk. The regal nature of eagle, the manoeuvrability of goshawk in woodland and after having spent the summer of '95 studying marsh and montagu harrier in Belarus, I certainly have a great affection for harriers. But for sure

Buzzard takes the prize for me every time. It could also be the fact that when I walked the West Highland Way with my son, they became the symbol for what the was the most amazing time we could have had, and if something gains an emotional attachment then its value increases by an unquantifiable amount. Especially if its quality time spent with a loved one.

It maybe the connection to a time long past, the fact that every message I have ever perceived from buzzard has been of great value. It maybe that I see them as the 'ford escort' of birds of prey, the base model that all other raptors have evolved from, the eagle grew, the kestrel shrunk so that it had the strength to hover, and the peregrine so that it could rise to great heights and fall faster than any other creature on the Earth, the osprey adapted so that it could catch fish from our lakes and seas. But buzzard stayed as buzzard. It could just be that I can sometimes see them from my back garden. As I have said above, and have often been heard to say, 'a buzzard day is always a good day!'

Whatever, watching a buzzard in the sky is a wondrous sight, they are a big, fairly solid looking bird that seems very at home in the skies, often the large wings, spanning about 1.2 metres in width never seem to be unnecessary used as they glide utilising thermals to keep them aloft or lift them higher effortlessly. A very efficient way to travel. They gently tilt to turn corners often circling in the sky. Whilst watching them you will notice how they hold their wings, almost level and perpendicular to their bodies, the primary feathers turning up at the end. When they do need to flap their wings, they do so in a lazy, effortless manner, utilising their massive wings to the full.

One of the ways a buzzard hunts is to use its very powerful eyesight, up to eight times better than a human, to search for prey on the ground which obviously it can see from a great distance. They will eat almost anything meaty; they are carnivores. Carrion is a favourite, it requires little energy, but they will take birds before they get to flight if they can, pigeons or partridges, but they are not especially skilled at this method of hunting, whilst successful enough to secure the wrath of many a gamekeeper in times past. They will take rabbits, or any other small creatures up to about 500g. Even taking large insects and worms when the opportunity presents itself.

Buzzards will also watch for prey whilst sat in trees and have even been known to chase prey whilst on the ground, albeit probably not their most successful hunting technique either, still when you are an opportunist.

As with all birds of prey, buzzards have RSSD. For the uninitiated, that is reverse size sexual dimorphism, which basically means the female is larger than the male. Seen together it's obvious, but in flight it's often the larger female that has primary feathers that span out into fingers and the smaller male that has what appear to be more 'solid' wings. Again, seen together it's obvious. The female is generally up to 10% bigger than the male which is quite a significant difference. It is probably an evolutionary development, which is likely to have been an early adaptation due to all raptors having it. It maybe because the female has more to do in defence of the nest and young, or the stamina required to incubate and lay her eggs. It may even be to provide a difference in the prey between the sexes and further reduce any competition for food.

Buzzards stay together for life and are extremely territorial when it comes down to the nesting area, each pair will often have up to around 20 nest sites available to them. The nests are about 1m in diameter usually in a tree, but other sites have been utilised. There are 2-4 eggs laid at three to four day intervals. The eggs are incubated for approximately 33 days. The female will stay on the nest for approximately 2 weeks until the chicks can defend themselves and tolerate any inclement weather. They will fledge at approximately 50 to 55 days old, and the parents will care and teach them for another 6 to 8 weeks.

Have you ever watched family groups flying around together in the autumn? They are a magnificent sight as they play in the air, the adults encouraging the youngsters to develop the skills they will need if they are to survive onto adulthood. Learning through play is the same for all species that actually raise their young on this planet.

These skills can be seen in the mating or strengthening courtship dance of the males in spring. They will rise majestically into the air, wings beating with purpose and definition, before dramatically gliding back to the lower skies, twisting and turning like a World War two fighter pilot as they go. Either winning the female or reminding her why she chose him in the first place.

Many juveniles will not make it to adulthood, the rigours of surviving in the wild can be tough, many dying either through starvation or competition. Ultimately, as long as each pair manage to be succeeded by a pair of birds of either sex the population will remain stable, and that's the important thing.

I mentioned above that watching buzzards in the sky is the most magic of natural wonders, but it's also important for another reason. Buzzards are top predators. Food chains and webs are discussed in Chapter 15, but having the birds that are at the top of the food chain in our skies is also an indicator of how good the rest of the food chain is doing. If any of the prey animals in the chain are missing the bird at the top of the food chain will be the first hit and will either starve or move on. So, the fact that buzzards are now our most commonly seen bird of prey all across the UK is a bit special. In the first instance it means that we are managing our world pretty well for the most part, and that is pretty reassuring, but it's also special because in the sixties, they were in danger, along with the majority of our raptors, of becoming extinct. Having survived persecution by landowners and gamekeepers during the 19th and early 20th centuries, they were making a fairly steady recovery, especially during World War Two, when attention was elsewhere.

They also managed to survive a massive explosion of myxomatosis during the fifties which wiped out a large part of their diet, only to be hit hard, as stated above by the extensive use of organochlorines (DDT) during the 60's. As ever not enough study was completed to ascertain the side effects of these chemicals before their widespread use to produce 'better' crops. What actually happened was that as the chemical made its way up the food chain, the amount in each animal increased until at the top, the levels were significant. Although it appeared to have no effect on the adults what it did do was reduce the thickness of the shells on the eggs the female gestated, meaning that the eggs couldn't survive the laying process and therefore most eggs were broken before they could even be laid and incubated. The life cycle destroyed before it even began. Population numbers plummeted.

Thankfully due to people pressure, research and observation the use of these chemicals was stopped and slowly our birds of prey managed to recover. The Buzzard especially well, and it has now recovered well enough to become our most common bird of prey. These large birds of prey, bodies of approximately half a metre and a wingspan of approximately 1.2 metres once again adorn our skies.

So, when you hear one, they sound remarkably similar to seagulls when they are calling, but unmistakable once that call is recognised, look to the skies and search for a large brown bird. Large enough, that you are hardly likely to misidentify it. It's large and it's brown. If it appears to have markings on its wings a bit like the roundels on a World War two spitfire fighter plane, then you've got a buzzard your sights.

Celebrate and enjoy the miracle that is the king (or Queen) of our skies. A bird that has been to the brink of extinction and made it back in spite of humankind. A symbol of times past and of bright awesome futures to come.

Did I mention I was a bit of a fan...

Chapter Nine.

On a Tuesday night in Sandwich in the summer they play cricket

In the middle of any bustling town there are quiet places. The way to find them, if you don't know them, is to go and look.

How do I know? Because that's just what we did once, although that wasn't the plan. I had suggested to my wife that we take Scruffy (our dog) around the Rope Walk in Sandwich.

The afternoon was chilly, so I had shut the kitchen doors when I began to prep the food. On her haphazard arrival, bag flung down, shawl lobbed, lady like, at the clothes hook, she began tidying, a sure sign that the day had not been entirely 'usual'.

'Can we eat outside?' She stated rather than asked.

'Absolutely', I replied.

A short while later and we 're in the car and on the way to Sandwich. We park up at the quay. There's a medieval toll gate and a car park next to the river Stour. The path begins parallel to the river going straight, with weeping willows between it and the river, huge, majestic trees that have inspired poets since time immemorial. Superb to sit below sheltering from the sun and listening to the wind as it blows through making the leaves rustle. On the right the ground drops away from the path. As a child I used to love riding off the edge and then trying to ride back up again. There's a play area in the same place as when I was young, but all the swings and roundabouts have changed now. There used to be a half circle 'arch' which was just high enough to be really scary to climb over. You had to turn around at the top to avoid coming down head first on the other side, that was scary too.

The path divides, straight on to follow Vigo Sprong, the name for the ditch dug out from the river, lovely old name don't you think. But we go right to follow the old town wall and cross over the bridge on Sandown Road. Again, when I was a child we used to ride our pushbikes under the bridge and try to surprise each other on the other side. A sign of the times I suppose it's now been blocked and a wall built, safety issue maybe, seems a shame.

The path rises and follows the back of the gardens of the houses on Knightrider Street to the right. You get glimpses of grand gardens and grand garden schemes the like of which most of us will only ever get to dream about. On the left, through the gaps in the trees, sycamores, elder and beech, you can see pasture and cows, lazily chewing the grass. Literally just off the centre of town, delightful.

As we round the corner there are paths that fan out from the ropewalk, as if they were spokes in a wheel that didn't stop at the rim. They begin as bridges that span the drop of what was once the moat outside the town wall forming part of the towns defences. Again, as a child they were great climbing frames, and for me much more fun than the endless rope swings that scared me witless. I can just about do heights now, but back then if there wasn't something solid between me and the ground, well....

A little further and there is Sandwich bowls club. You can see the square of immaculately prepared grass, perfectly flat, green, very manicured, with members of the club playing said game. A scene so English, possibly second only to cricket, and a likely album for cover for 70's prog band Genesis. Remember them?

128

But ultimately, it's people enjoying the outside for recreation, and why not, there's even a bench up on the rope walk so you can sit and watch. It's a slow gentle activity and just being next to it and letting it's ambience wash over you will help you slow your mind. If you stop to 'observe' what else is around you, you will likely hear the songs of birds. Blackbirds are a frequent caller on a summer evening, in fact, for me, their song is evocative of a summer evening. Maybe insects buzzing or crickets rubbing their back legs together, almost reminiscent of how the African savannah might sound, after all it's all a version of nostalgia and romance. A mind job for ourselves.

We walk on, and as we approach New Street, we stop Scruffy and put him on the lead. He's quite good at stopping and crossing the road to heal, but he's got a bit enthusiastic lately and so we don't take any chances. Letting him off as we enter the next section of path. Here to the left is a section of moat that is still very much effective as it is full of water. I have had some great times fishing there in the past. There are avenues of trees either side of the path, beeches, yews and a lot of limes too. A walnut stands proud at the end of the bank, scruffy was running and bounding around them like a fresh spring lamb, full of the joy of just being alive.

Have you ever watched butterflies as they roll and tumble along a hedgerow? They look like they are having the time of their lives, as they roll and chase and flit up and down, their colours becoming a blur. A few years ago, we had amassed invasion from Europe of thousands upon thousands of small tortoiseshell butterflies. There were so many they almost blanketed fields. Watching them performing their aerial acrobatics is a heart-warming sight, somehow everything feels good in the world, whatever you're feeling.

I doubt that butterflies do 'happy' or have any real concept of it, but they certainly look like they do!

So, back to the plot, after we cross Woodnesborogh Road, the ropewalk becomes the Butts, the moat continues after we leave the road and willows once again line the bank. There are couples and families enjoying the new born warmth, we pass the car park of the towns supermarket on the right full of the sounds of cars arriving and departing and the chatter of shoppers having stocked up for the week.

But the most prominent sound is the one of a hard cricket ball getting struck by a cricket bat. It's one of those sounds that is quintessentially English, even though it's heard all over the world. A sound that has a huge dollop of satisfaction, just like an arrow hitting a boss. Donk!!!

But watching a cricket match, with all the players in their 'whites', the bowler running up to the crease, hoping his next bowl will unsettle or fool the batsman into getting himself out, or staring aghast as he hits the ball once again for a six is pure English summer, as much as ratty taking the shy and quiet mole for a punt down the river.

The cricketers' wives having tea and cucumber sandwiches ready for supper. Personally, I think cucumber sandwiches are disgusting, but you can't paint that picture without them.

Just to add in a little reality, we haven't brought a pooh bag, we normally walk out in the middle of nowhere where the need is not so great. We have been stopping scruffy performing that deed all along the walk and retrieve an empty bread bag from the bin. 'Really?' you ask, 'yes, really.' And do you know what else? Now we have a bag he doesn't poo again, or even try to. Life is...

We reach the end of the path at Strand Street, just passed some lovely little cottages that have watched the world turn ever so gently and still have no road at their door and again we are reminded that there are some wonderful quiet and calm places in our own little world and right on our own doorstep if we just get out and look.

We've had a lovely gentle little walk, seen life doing its own thing by many different people and birds and insects that we would have missed had we stayed in and turned on the television, a device that shows us wonderful things and isolates us from them at the same time.

What do we do? Well, we could turn right and walk along the road, passed large houses full of grandeur and history. Fine examples of Tudor and Georgian and Victorian history, with Scruffy on the lead as the cars rush passed us, but no, we turn round and keep that air of peace, calm and gentle activity of both ourselves and others. We retrace our steps hand in hand as we wander the long way back the quay and our car.

Chapter ten.

Infrequent islands of time (2019)

<u>Friday.</u>

Infrequent islands of time. Like the sound of that phrase. Conjures up a world of possibilities, both real and imagined. Here I am once again in Port Zelande in Holland, and the oasis of calm that is the 'marillion' weekend. I have been here on three previous occasions, in 07, 09 and 15. 07 was my boys mums 40th and 09 was because 07 was good and then real life got in the way. And as with 15, Helen and Paul are here with us, we're sharing a chalet this time, Helen and Gillian get on really well and ultimately, why not? Hence, infrequent islands of time.

I thought I'd bring the laptop and see what I might write while we were here, 4 years after the last time. A lot has happened since then, if you've read the first book you'll know! I guess the trick for me is not to repeat myself too much.

So, since 2015 some very important events occurred; I got separated from my boys mother, Gillian and I became an item, got engaged, I then got divorced and got married again, in that order. Released the first book, sold a fair few copies too, became a fairly prolific public speaker and got banned from the Women's Institute as a speaker, renegade that

I am. Split the business in two in an effort to avoid VAT registration. Got registered for VAT. Have now four employees, finally got a website that works. Still keep getting dragged back onto the tools, but that is becoming rarer. But the business plan that kept setting more and more 'realistic' targets is finally starting to hit them. Keep chasing those dreams.

It's funny, in the lead up to the weekend work had been so busy all I wanted to do was 'just get on the ferry'. Managed that, left the work phone with Soph and deleted the e mail app from my phone. Just peace quiet, chilling out and marillion for five days. Bliss. And then my senior op gets into a 'handbags at dawn' scene with a clients' neighbour and the rest of the team have formed a supportive cordon around him. I have also had two potential clients get in touch through Facebook, the delivery I scheduled for Friday is coming Saturday and no one is about to meet it or sign for it, (turns out they have delivered one screen of the wrong type), best laid plans and all that: you can't easily totally isolate yourself from the world of business these days. Still, nothing I can do in Holland and thankfully I am pretty good at detachment these days and have inadvertently managed to pretty much box the last of the anxiety issues that had lingered from all the other stuff I wrote about in the last book.

There are always 'firsts' and we have a few here. Obviously, the first marillion weekend with Gillian. And as I'm prone to saying, that is 'cool' in itself, but also a first, I am alcohol free (AF). As I write this, I am on day 47, over halfway through a ninety-day challenge. Several times over the last 18 months I had threatened to give up alcohol, but always let myself get talked out of it. 'Phew,' I would think, politics played well again. There have been several incidents where I have let alcohol get the better of me, some mentioned in the last book and others since. But the one that finally gave me realisation that enough is enough was at our works do in December, and another one that's a first, normally these do's are between Christmas and the New Year.

Anyway, the event itself was a great success and the majority of people went home about elevenish, Gillian sent me to make sure one of our staffers had got home ok, bottle of rum in, did that OK came home and decided to drink whiskey in fairly large amounts. My favourite whiskey too, Laphroaig, which I only drink in small doses, for flavour. Half a bottle later, and let's get this into perspective, whiskey on top of a couple of beers, some red wine and sloe gin at a minimum, I decided to take Scruffy for a walk. I returned however long later, without Scruffy.

I awoke next morning less than popular with my nearest and dearest and had no recollection as to why. This had to stop. For the first time in my life, I knew I had to change my relationship with alcohol. Not for those around me, but for me. That is the key, not for anyone else. Me, me with a capitol M.

I think that is the vital component with making any change of this nature and probably why so many fail; you can't give up for anyone else, or for anything else, it has to be because you really want to, right to the core of your very being. There is a huge difference between knowing you should give up and actually wanting to. It took me four years between initial realisation and the latter. When I finally got to that point with smoking it was easy, well as easy as it can be. I didn't give it up, it just wasn't something I did any more. And now I'm the same with alcohol. There are still times when I want a beer, but the answers 'no'. Unequivocally. It does help that there are some really cool tasting AF beers. And sometimes you need a flavour that is not tea or soft drinks. It's great when you go out for a meal or to the pub because you are the only one who can drink two and still drive, ha ha!!!

I will get back to the positives later, but this is a great place to include this change because the marillion weekend had the potential to be a real challenge. Four nights where I would feel like I should be drinking. Although that became easier than I expected.

A few weeks back we had an eighties night to attend. And I guess that needs a bit of a back story too, because it has an impact on the story of the alcohol-free weekend that this trip to Port Zelande has become. I do hope you're keeping up.

So, eighties night, we had to go because it became a fund raiser that we could piggyback onto the new 'younger' Rotary club that I in advertently found myself figure heading. Sorry, but you're not getting the back story on that one, this is not the Two Ronnie's. But one of the principle components of Rotary Clubs is to fund raise and one of our 'members' was organising said eighties night and was prepared to let us keep 50% of any tickets we sold, so we had to go. And go we did. I drank AF beer for most of the night. Tasted a bit weird, but I have drunk beer with alcohol that tasted just like it. After three I reverted back to blackcurrant and lemonade and was almost relieved to do so. Funnily enough the beer was called Nanny State, I think the brewers were having a laugh.

One of the bonus' of being sober is drunk watching which can be highly entertaining. One lady was hammered and wanted to dance with everybody, especially the blokes and appeared to be looking to find one to get amorous with, failing each time, moving onto the next potential candidate. Anyway, I digress, whilst everyone else was drinking, Gillian commented later that I looked very content sober. And I was too. I think one of the most difficult things with not drinking is that we are so programmed that we should drink on so many occasions that we feel like we are missing out if we are not. You know, 'I've had a bad day, I deserve a drink', 'I've had a good day, I deserve a drink', I had a tough day, I deserve a drink' etc. Any excuse is utterly justified. Not the case I can assure you.

You may remember from above that I had mentioned above that this evening was significant, and it was. After that night Paul decided, for reasons of his own that he also was going to go AF for a while, and he seems to be doing really well with it too. And for this weekend, well it is much easier with two, for sure. Big call.

<u>Saturday.</u>

I love the way that marillion manage to keep inventing new ways of packaging their music for the weekends because they know that everyone there will probably know all their back catalogue. We were treated to four mini gigs based on the first four albums with the new singer. I should add he's only been there for 30 years now but most of the rest of the world still thinks original singer Fish is still there. They also played tracks that might not usually be the first choice for performance. That's the beauty of these weekend festivals, they are basically just glorified love ins...

One thing that never changes though is the size of the fans that seem to surround us, we always seem to find the local rugby teams pack, six and a half feet at a minimum. We did not have the greatest view for most of the evening. It was also cool to join in with the drunks and raise my arms in the air, jump about and sing and clap with the best of them whilst sober. Cheaper too and I will remember everything the next day.

And that is one of the things that I love about sobriety, waking up clear headed in the morning. I often use it to diffuse a trigger when I want a drink the night before.

It has to be said that apart from the obvious haziness, which is great if you can control it, and as I'm finding out I'm not that good at that anymore, I'm not actually seeing a downside to 'not' drinking. And I'll spell it out.

- As I said waking up refreshed. And alive, really alive.
- Knowing exactly what I've done the night before. Even remembering the end of movies.
- Not talking rubbish or being abusive, or randomly repeated myself.
- Shedding loads of inherent anxiety, I never realised just how much of a depressant alcohol is.

- I am waking up remembering dreams, you can't live with part of your thinking being locked up in a box and not allowing you to reach anything like your full potential. My subconscious can now bolster my conscious mind. This is probably why so many of the worlds very successful people increasingly drink very little.
- Realising just how much society is driven by blocking out half our lives with haziness, to the point where not knowing what we're doing is to be boasted about. Is it really about control? We had a client who had been ill for over a fortnight. We rocked up on site on a Saturday morning and when he appeared in a dressing gown at maybe tenish, when I asked him how he was he replied, 'well enough to drink beer'. Inside I thought 'really?!?' with a frown.
- It's possible I've lost half a stone.
- I've definitely saved a lot of money, definitely over £280.00 in the first month because that's how much I had to pay for the last instalment to come here. As a ready reckoner, average a couple of bottles of beer and a bottle of wine between the two of us and possibly more at a weekend, that's about £15.00 per night, Wednesday, Friday, Saturday and Sunday, say four times a month, so £60.00 a week and £240.00 A MONTH. Just think what you can do with that money...
- But the real payoff is watching my wife relax around me, and really relax. Not having to watch out for any mood changes or disappointments that might trigger me off, even sober. And that works both ways, because I haven't let myself down, my guards down too, so I make better choices and when Gillian does the things that might have set me off I just grin, because I know I've not done anything to deserve a jibe. And we both enjoy intimate silliness that you just can't have unless you're totally comfortable with each other.

Do I seriously want to give up all this for a few hours of drunk enhanced 'happiness'?

(Alcohol is a drug, so a little bit of me does, like having a cigarette, but...)

And there are some slightly daft advantages too...

- You don't spend half your outings worried about who's going to drive because you must have a beer, and the night won't be fun if you can't have one.
- You can have a real session and if you run out of beer then you can just drive to the supermarket and buy some more.
- No one wants to nick your beer at parties, although on the occasion they do, their horror when it is pointed out it's AF is priceless. Beer with no alcohol??? Rather drink acid.

I joined an online challenge group One Year No Beer. I enrolled in the ninety-day challenge. They have a 28-day challenge, but I figured I'd be just waiting until I could start drinking again, a bit like dry January. That wasn't going to change the relationship I had with alcohol. Ninety it had to be. You are supposed to set yourself a challenge, but my knees are rubbish and I'm not really a swimmer, but I did manage to find a reward for myself if I made it. IF? Not really an option, there are challenges to come but as I said, ultimately, I don't want to drink. There's a 365-day challenge too, not sure about that at the moment. Questions are, can I moderate? And do I want to?

To be fair, the challenge was mostly for other people. I knew I was going to stop drinking. The decision was made, but people don't want others to stop drinking. The cajoling and provocation can be remorseless and unremitting.

Anyway, back to that reward. There have been three really cool albums to come out this year, a new 'bring me the horizon' album and a new Dream Theater album, but most importantly back then the Within Temptation album called 'Resist'. It had a basic concept of not letting

138

the pressures of society make you anything other than what you are. It had a fantastic futuristic sleeve too. Most importantly the music was exceptionally good as well, awesome album. It should have arrived just before I made the decision to go alcohol free; the first CD never made it, I got a refund and ordered it again, that saved me eight quid, so I ordered another album to go with it. The second attempt at the album arrived a week later. That kind of fitted too, nothing worth having is ever easy. That is not actually true, but we like to tell ourselves that the case. I had planned on having the title in the graphic that it is on the album as a tattoo, but that wasn't completely right either, until the t shirt I bought arrived and I saw the logo in the mirror. Now that worked, wasn't cheesy and meant an awful lot to me. Sorted. In fact, in the end, I actually mirrored the image, combined the t's and put it on the inside of my right forearm. I will carry a symbol of my sobriety on my arm for ever.

There was also a big amount of karma involved, the main theme of the last book was all about taking responsibility for your actions and ultimately, I knew my behaviour was not good. And I was not taking responsibility for that. Like the song says, 'sometimes want you want is not what you need', thanks Mr Martin. This also is a real benefit of not drinking.

The following is a post I put on the Facebook forum for OYNB

'Day 42, becoming alcohol free is a bit like leaving 'the matrix'. I'm sure you've seen the film.

One brave decision opens a whole new fantastic reality. Why would you want to go back to the numb haziness of lost hours and days?

Life is precious, live it.'

And right now, we are waiting for tonight's gig, what will it be. Dunno, but I know I'll remember it...

<u>Monday.</u>

Never got time to write yesterday. Here we are in the chalet still. We have to be out by ten, but there's no rush. The ferry crossing has been delayed by an hour and a half, so we will have about three hours to fill, which will probably be spent back in Bruges. We had an excellent lunch there on the way in, which feels so long ago now.

We are experiencing that strange emotion that we always feel when a fantastic time away from the normality of life is coming to an end. Especially if you have a little time to kill. And so different from the moment I described earlier when all I wanted to do was get on the ferry, with the whole weekend still in front of us. I remember the excitement as you drive along the coast road towards Port Zelande and you can see the tent from a few miles away.

That tent is a very important tent, it is only there for a couple of weeks every couple of years and signifies that marillion are in town. It's big enough to hold a stage and everything that goes with that as well as three thousand people, a massive bar and obviously toilets too, thus, it can be seen for miles around. So, as I said 'a very important tent'.

I think I said in the last book, it's important to sit down at the beginning of any adventure and acknowledge that it's all still to come and this is the beginning, and this was the moment, for me, to do that.

What followed were three nights of very intense and emotional music spanning the 30 years that 'new' singer 'H' had been in the band and with all the stupidity of Brexit in the air, a major example of how all people can exist together in some magical sense of harmony. This wasn't missed, dare I say, by anyone in attendance at all.

One of the questions we discussed was how much of the vegetation was here before the area became a Centre Park? And of interest because the vegetation is right up to the chalets, but not densely, and so wildlife is right around you too, from mallard ducks to robins and great tits primarily. Other kinds of animal too I suspect, some being more secretive, and this as you'll know always interests me greatly. The whole area is part of a nature reserve, Port Zelande is a peninsula and largely surrounded by sea. We walked all around it on the Friday morning and through the fog, which gave the place an eerie beauty we saw, greylag geese, swans, herons, and cormorants to name a few. In the Market dome, shopping/café centre of the resort they have turtles, fish, and a couple of flamingos. You don't see them every day of the week.

It's also funny, I have always fancied staying at the Centre around the weekend, well, it would have to be the week before really. I don't think I could handle it without the constant stream of marillion music through all, and I mean ALL speakers everywhere, marillion logos on all paper ware from menus, to tickets, to signs and even on the TV, the vibe is just so cool, permanent, but not invasive. Like I said above, a bit of a love in...

It was sad to see the tent in the process of being dismantled as we left.

You always know how good a gig, or this weekend is by the amount of time you keep playing the music of said artist. Once again, I think it may be a while...

One other huge positive was that I am now totally cool with AF beers, still don't want to have too many because they cost the same as beer with alcohol, but ultimately why not.

Another realisation, and this is another unqualified thought; we have a kind of base level state of happiness that we experience highs and lows based upon. When we start drinking as teenagers that is where we rise from and enjoy that alcohol induced high, but as we continue drinking into adulthood our base level drops and we need alcohol to get to where our base level once was, and that is before we even get a high, hence the phrase, 'god I need a drink!' When we stop drinking it doesn't take long for our bodies to remember normality and we wonder why we ever needed to drink the quantities we are encouraged too.

Certainly my wife will tell you I have been far more likely to dance at parties and get involved in activities way outside my old comfort zone, dressing up as a pirate to promote our treasure hunt or entering a strictly come dancing event spring to mind.

Back to blue pill red pill...

I put another post up on the OYNB site yesterday and it very much fits with the no alcohol and marillion theme, I'll paraphrase it to make it fit properly, but basically...

Marillion played their album 'happiness is the road' almost in its entirety on the Sunday, the reality being that the journey is more fun than the destination and for most of our endeavours in life I believe this is totally true. The joy of achievement can be short lived, and we need to set ourselves on a new journey or target to aim for. With alcohol the opposite is true. The journey is tortuous, especially for the people around us. Happiness on this particular journey is very definitely at the end of the road, we just don't know it until we actually put our feet on the road. The journey is fraught with difficulty and wrong choices and imposed pressures, the threat of renewed oblivion ever present. Just like the butterfly coming out of its cocoon, the alcohol-free new world is an amazing place. Time to enjoy.

So back home and back into action. I think I am going to have to hit the ground running tomorrow...

Oh, and Scruffy, despite Ross, my son, and his mates going to look for him, he wandered back by himself in his usual way, when he was ready. And probably oblivious to the chaos surrounding our little jaunt.

Post Script, May 2021.

One of the most important 'things' in life has to be at peace with yourself. That is best achieved by always being aware of yourself, your surroundings, your actions. That can only be achieved by being aware of where you are, what you are doing, thinking and saying. That can only be achieved by being in a natural state of being.

I do have a glass of wine, a glass of whiskey, or a beer when I wish to. Sometimes I drink a lot of alcohol-free beer, although not very often. Sometimes I have been more than a little tipsy on just one drink, and others find that amusing.

Fuzzy is the time to stop; I have no desire to be fuzzy at all.

It also occurs to me now, we were never meant to view this world, this utterly amazing world we are fortunate enough to live in through alcohol fogged eyes. It is impossible to feel connected, balanced and centred through an altered perception of reality.

My relationship with alcohol has changed utterly.

I am at peace.

Chapter eleven.

Swarm

Back in the dark mists of time, well about ten years ago I used to operate as a handyman. Before that is, I decided to specialise in one thing and make everything as simple as possible. I had not long taken on a member of staff; I had an enthusiastic new assistant. It was a Saturday, and we were working for a regular client on the local estate. Country estate that is, not a local new housing estate.

I had worked for these good people for quite a while at this time and done various different tasks as required. They had a colony of bees nesting in the cavity of one of their walls. The wall that was unfortunately right next to the window of the nursery. They had wanted the bees gone, for fear of the young lad getting stung. A worthy if uneducated opinion.

It is common for people to have the idea that all insects that can sting you, will sting you. And then sometimes to quantify that statement, by saying that if it's a bee it won't sting you because it will die, but a wasp will want to sting you and they won't die.

This is all a lot of mumbo jumbo to be honest. Bees won't sting you unless they have a reason and whilst it is possible for a bee to sting you and live it is unlikely, they have barbs on their sting and if these penetrate the victim's skin they cannot be pulled out. Occasionally they will sting you with little penetration. Wasps have no barbs and so can sting you repeatedly. Some are very aggressive too. Generally though, as with bees if you don't flap at them, they won't sting you either. Why would they? What have they got to gain? Nothing. They don't have any axe to grind or hold grudges. There is no advantage to a wasp in stinging you.

That said though, the only person I know who did get stung by these bees was me. Whilst mowing. If the bees are harvesting flowers found on a lawn such as daisies, or buttercups for example they will be hovering all over the ground as they do in late summer, then you are going to disturb bees that are focussed on the job at hand, when mowing.

Whilst all bees collect nectar and pollen and make honey to some extent, it's only the honey bee that produces honey in large enough quantities to make it worth harvesting.

Male bees do virtually no work and thus are not 'produced' in large numbers. Most bees are females, who do pretty much all the work, half the time foraging and collecting pollen and nectar, the other half working on the hive. Each adult lives for approximately 6 weeks, but honey bee hives are perennial compared to the bumble bee where only the queens over winter.

What's really amazing though, (apart from the fact that they fly at all, see chapter 15) is the way they communicate to each other where to go and find honey. Put simply, when a bee finds a great source of pollen and nectar they fly back to the colony and perform a waggle dance. The waggle dance is a figure of eight. The bee waggles whilst moving through the middle section each time she returns to it. That line through the middle of the eight is the direction of the honey. The length of time the bee spends in the 'waggle' is proportional to the distance away.

Incredible innate skill for an insect that lives for just six weeks. And a talent that may quite possibly determine the survival of the hive!

Another incredibly amazing thing about the life cycle of honey bees is the swarm. It's an important part of the reproductive cycle. A queen bee will lay queen eggs in special cells. The workers will then stop feeding her. As a result, she will stop laying eggs. She cannot fly if too heavy. When she leaves the colony, she has only the food she can carry with her, as do the workers that go with her, so often bees will already have worked out where they will begin a new colony when they swarm. This usually a spring behaviour.

Now, have you ever seen a bee swarm? It is unbelievable, a real sensory overload. I have only ever seen it once, and I imagine the story has got bigger with each retelling. Here is the current version.

As I said, it was a Saturday, in spring, in the afternoon. We were tidying up the garden, nearing completion. I was chatting with our client just outside the doorway on a small patio, my assistant was rounding up all the green waste. It was warm and calm, a balmy spring afternoon.

Bees had been going to and fro from the usual spot in the cavity and all seemed as normal at first, no one took any special notice of the activity. Then there seemed to be a few more bees coming from the cavity, but again, nothing greatly out of the ordinary, activity began to escalate and we began to notice that there were quite a lot of bees congregating, and then an awful lot of bees began appearing and clustering and before we knew it there was a massive ball of bees, probably about a metre in diameter. I always like to say it was 2 metres in diameter, but I don't think there would've been enough room in the cavity for that many bees, and besides a great story always gets better with the telling. Even so, a metre in diameter means there must have been hundreds, if not thousands of bees.

Can you just imagine it, a living breathing moving, pulsing ball of life? Each representative of that life has the ability to sting you, and if they wanted to, with that many stings they could kill you. If they had the desire to. Fortunately, at this time they were not interested in us at all. Not one bit. We were utterly irrelevant to the single intention from any or all of the bees. Certainly, as long as we didn't attract attention. They were all totally focussed on the queen and what she was up to. My client called her husband to come and observe this most awesome of natural spectacles that was happening quite literally on her doorstep.

My assistant however was not quite holding this swarm in the same awe that we were. Awe probably, but probably, mostly, awe based on fear. He couldn't get far enough away from them. To him they were just bugs that bit you. He seriously adjusted his view of the natural world whilst he worked with me. Even got excited about some of it on some occasions.

But there was one other factor that was even more jaw droppingly awesome. The sheer volume of that many bees buzzing all in one place at the same time. Imagine, if you will, one bee buzzing, and then magnify that by a thousand, or maybe two. Buzzing on another level.

Loud!

Really loud.

I mean having to shout above it loud.

And maybe just two or three metres away

Not that you wanted to shout or do anything to disrupt this amazing spectacle.

I have never seen or heard anything like it since either.

It was loud!

I don't know how long the bees stayed like that, just flying together in a ball, buzzing, it seemed like ages, but was probably only a minute or so. But then they split into two balls, literally about five metres apart. Now we've got bees buzzing in stereo. They seemed even louder. Turn off one of the speakers on your stereo, you'll see (hear) what I mean, well, in reverse.

Then, almost on cue, both swarms returned to the wall and the cavity. In seconds. With more precision and organisation than an army could organise. The original half of the swarm to where it came from, and the 'new' swarm to a mirror image location the other side of the door.

And all of a sudden, the world was silent.

An eerie silence.

Made most noticeable because of the sheer volume of the massive swarms we had just experienced had gone, and gone so quickly.

After a mutual acknowledgement, we all turned and went back to whatever tasks we had been attending to before a natural wonder had changed us all, at least just a little bit.

Chapter 12.

The Unexpected Grey Seals

Chris Williams had posted on Facebook in the morning, his post had been vaguely scientific about why we should venture outside and the benefits of luminescence to the human soul. We need daylight to feel awake and that as light decreases the body prepares itself for sleep and rest. Just getting outside for 15 – 30 minutes is vital for our general health and wellbeing.

I posted a reply, 'Absolutely agree, my whole philosophy in anything I do'. Grammar could've been better, but...

I know this to my core but sometimes it can become abundantly obvious even to seriously hardened converts such as myself. Let me explain further.

Today is Wednesday January 2nd, 2019. I am on a short holiday with my wife. After a fantastic, but busy Christmas with our mostly local, but well spread-out family we had absconded to Norfolk for a few days, the brief was to have a quiet New Year, just walk the dog, read books, watch box sets, write a little; for myself this book and Gillian had a quiz and one or two other things she needed to do. Scruffy, the dog, overdoses on loves and cuddles too.

As, dare I say, successful business people we find this very hard to do at home. There is always something to attend to and as we don't very often get lots of time together just for the two of us, we tend to grab a week here and there to just live untidily and do lazy stuff. Has to be said, if we lived like this at home, we'd give ourselves a good talking to.

And we have been successful too, I've read a whole book; in two days, watched several movies, the box set was a disaster, walked around the gentle countryside. I have written half of a more challenging chapter and had the most sobrietous New Year ever, well as an adult, the only unexpected difficulty has been waking up on New Year's Eve with an uncomfortable knee. I get aches and pains on a fairly regular basis as a result of middle age and an occasionally very physical job, so I thought little of it, and we duly went and walked a very pleasant three or four miles.

As the evening progressed the joint began to swell and seize up and I had a fairly uncomfortable night, waking every time I turned over. New Year's Day we did very little, rose late, watched Notting Hill, I had forgotten what a gem of a movie it is, read a magazine and generally just chilled for the day.

As my wife pointed out when we awoke today, I'd had a fairly rough night, I wasn't awake a lot, but regularly. Have to assume I'd woken her a fair amount too. Not to worry we got up and had breakfast, Gillian had found some decaying heat treatment that she rubbed into my knee, it either made a great difference or just numbed the pain, not sure which, but as the plan was to go to Winterton on Sea and get a flavour of the Norfolk east coast we stuck with Plan A.

On arrival in Winterton we grabbed a cuppa, vital when you've run out of milk, (how did we allow that to happen?) and went to the car park on the coast. We sat in the car to enjoy our drinks and observed that the car park was full and wondered why, with this many people about, the café on the beach was shut. We may have left our businesses at home but still can't stop thinking like business folk.

Anyway, beverages finished we kitted up and headed for the dunes. Scruff was beside himself with happiness with some real outdoor freedom and was charging around like some crazed dervish. As we passed the wardens huts two wardens came passed carrying a bag, seemed insignificant at the time. Just passed the huts Gillian realised she had left her phone in the car and returned to collect it. At the pace I was hobbling I wasn't going to get very far ahead.

The dunes were a typical mix of sandy passages and marram grasses so typical of English Dunes, but untypically to the right was a fairly steep drop. I wanted to get down to vast expanses of sand that divided the upper dune terrace I was on and the sea. There was no obvious way down, until I spotted a 'gash' in the 'cliff' face. I seriously considered the wisdom of descending through it, especially with this uncooperative knee. I just as briefly considered how I might get back up, but only briefly as I descended, operating a balance of consideration for my abilities, with my desires. I'd worry about that later. I then thought where's Scruff? He was there a moment earlier but had vanished. He reappeared as usual and charged straight down the bank clearly without any hesitation at all. And proceeded to carry on madly charging about as if his mere existence depended upon it. Life affirming in itself, we can, I feel, learn a lot form dogs....

It was at this point that Gillian reappeared. "Down there?' she enquired, knowing the answer. I smiled. As she joined us, we held hands and headed across the flats. We were well wrapped up; the wind was blowing with plenty of venom from the North. But despite the chill, the sun was shining, Scruffy was still charging about as his very existence depended upon it and everything was right with the world. It was one of those moments you cannot get indoors, I could feel my whole sense of being rise, a kind of mini euphoria that money can't buy. The feel of wind brushing passed me on its way to wherever, clean and fresh. A smell so fresh it makes your nose stand up and take attention, and eyes responding to the brightness of the day. The feel of sand underneath your boots, too cold today to take them off, but Scruff had no such worries. And don't forget the sea, the sound of it washing along any beach is calming and relaxing when gentle, but bracing when on a day like this. It has the wind to strengthen its resolve as waves crash upon the shore, to die and then be reborn for another assault.

Further proof that on this trip we/you acknowledge that the fact we are outside and our spirits have lifted and life is good, we just have to tune into it.

But that was not the whole story, not by any means. We carried on along the beach and the cliff reduced in scale until it was just another part of the system of dunes, so getting back to the car wasn't going to be too much of a challenge. As we progressed there was a collection of people up ahead, strange we thought. The nearer we got, and again we could see someone in a high viz vest; must be something going on then. As usual we scanned to see what was occurring with the dogs, they were all on a lead. Decided Scruffy was okay for the moment and left him loose. He's generally more interested in the dog walkers than the dogs.

There were some largish blobs on the sand.

'Do you think they are seals?' asked Gillian.

'No', I reply, 'they'd have a natural fear of humans, especially here, that is healthy.'

As we progress there is a partly eaten corpse of a baby dolphin. Odd. At this point we put Scruffy on the lead, discretion being the better part of valour.

As we get nearer to these blobs one of them moves. Wow, they are seals, I can hardly believe it, I have never been this close to a wild seal before, again Wow. They are large dark 'grey' seals and their almost light brown, white pups. And they are utterly unfazed by the number of people all around them. If the adults move it is to gently raise their heads, and maybe at a push to raise an eyebrow, they are so relaxed. But for the pups it is a different matter, they have only been here for a few weeks, or possibly even days and life for them is just so brand new.

Whilst seals are clumsy on land, they are cute too. Whether just raising their head and tail in some bizarre banana impression, or balancing on their tail and fore paws and bouncing along the beach around mum, inactivity is obviously much harder for them, and if there's another pup to play chase with... With all this love around them they don't realise just how good they've got it here.

We approach the warden and enquire politely about the seals, but as with every volunteer he just wants to tell us everything he can about the seals he so obviously loves. Grey seals come ashore to have their pups, they stay in close attendance for about three weeks, leave them largely to it for three weeks, making sure they have enough to eat before they all go to the sea after about 6 weeks. You have to wonder why they give birth to their pups at such a chilly time of year, but when you remember they have blubber enough to keep them warm in our even colder seas, a chill wind is probably of very little consequence.

They are supervised from a distance by the wardens who try to remain distant and separate to the wonder that is happening here, occasionally though they have to step in. The package I mentioned earlier, by the wardens' huts was a pup that had been attacked by some soulless dog owners dog. Do not get me started on that one.

There was also a pup that appeared to have been abandoned, if mum hadn't appeared by tomorrow then it would be taken to the RSPCA to be raised before getting returned to the wild. Interestingly mums' milk is rich enough for the pup to go to sea in six weeks, it will take the RSPCA 6 months. All jokes about mothers milk go here.

Incidentally, there are about 95,000 grey seals around the British coast, about 60% of the world's population, they only come ashore to give birth to their pups and generally prefer rockier locations or at least more deserted beaches than this one, so this is a bit more unusual, maybe though explains their lack of fear. Big up to the wardens I say.

There were flocks of small birds also abundant on the beach too. I'm not sure exactly what they were. I can tell you all the different bird species that they weren't. I only had an old pair of bins from our holiday cottage. They looked like buntings, or maybe finches, but the only bird I can find in my books that looks similar is snow buntings which do descend on the more northerly beaches of Norfolk in Winter, so that possibility that makes this trip even more special. Snow buntings join us in the winter migrating down from the arctic. They are browner in the winter, but the white is still prominent, especially in such a small bird.

The trip back to the car was much less eventful, but what an afternoon. We probably spent more time in the car getting there and back and walked far less than we might have done if I hadn't joined the ranks of hop alongs. But what an afternoon, it would have been awesome without the seals and buntings. But when you add in any creature that so obviously displays the joys of just being alive you can't help but let a little of that rub off on you. If you want to live in this world, then just be a part of it, and not apart from it!

Chapter 13.

Osprey

Ospreys are like that fella you know, you only see them rarely, but when you do, they never fail to seriously impress you. I mean just take a look at them visually in the first instance. Similar in length to a buzzard, but slimmer, with longer, more pointed wings. In colour they are more striking too, upper parts dark brown almost black even with white undersides, stippled with brown on the chest. But their head is unique. A dark strip across the eyes with a flecked crown or crest, making them look very regal. Most importantly powerful white legs and talons. Vital for any raptor, but especially so for osprey as we shall discuss later.

Osprey was a late addition to this text, but fits in with our theme of being alert of all life around us when out and about in our country side. Three occasions spring to mind. The first was when I was carrying out the practical work for my dissertation on Marsh and Montagu's harriers whilst in Belarus. Then, they were just a big bird identified by the local scientist overseeing our work. Difficult to stand out in amongst all the wonder I was experiencing of a different culture as well as over one hundred species of other birds, quite a few that were raptors. Obviously at the time the aerial magnificence of Marsh Harrier and the scarcity in the UK of Montagus Harrier took precedence in my fledgling fascination with birds.

Fast forward to 2021 and after just over a year in and out of lockdown due to the ongoing pandemic that is/was covid 19, my wife and I headed out for the holiday that we had booked last year and had to put on hold. To say it was a welcome break is an understatement. Whereas many good folk had been put on furlough, (told to stay at home on a basic level of pay), working for myself meant that I had rarely stopped. Most clients sucked me into their properties as if they were a vacuum and garden design seemed to be in fair demand throughout. The largest difference was having my wife and son home considerably more than they would have been otherwise.

In a normal world we'd have had 3 or 4 holidays a year. The sense of expectation through the build-up was unlike any other and difficult to explain. It was hard to believe we were actually going. Anywhere!

Clients could not believe we were actually going away either.

'You're staying at home, right?' they'd ask.

'No, we're going away.'

'On holiday?' they'd ask, incredulous.

'Yes, we'll be away.'

'Oh.'

I think they thought I just wasn't going to do their design.

However, depart we did, and whilst travelling along the A590 to our cottage in Coniston I saw a hand painted sign at the side of the road that said, 'ospreys' with an arrow pointing to the left. Needless to say, on that occasion we didn't go in, it had been a long day and we were knackered. For want of a better phrase.

However, we had to go back. Ospreys! It was just finding the time. Especially as we had to plan our outdoor activities with great care. It was likely to be raining for a large percentage of our holiday. So, on a day that probably wouldn't be too wet we set off for Lake Windermere, for a wander, the plan to go to Foulshaw Moss, as we had discovered the ospreys were currently residing, afterwards. Turned out there was another pair nesting somewhere else close by, but that wouldn't have been right would it?

On arrival we pulled into the small but perfectly formed car park and got seriously distracted by the goldfinches taking seed from the feeders. I'll never tire of the red and gold of these stunning little finches. It is a cold day, and I am glad I'm not the volunteer on duty in the gazebo at the entrance. We chat about osprey, and the reserve before wandering off down the boardwalked path between the trees to the observation tower. A metre or two high, the tower gives beautifully sparse views across the bog. Trees line the perimeter of the boggy area that is interspersed with pools. Without the boardwalk the whole place would be completely inaccessible. The Moss is full of Scotch heather around the margins with crossleaf heath taking over as you look further in. Tussock cotton grass is in clear evidence wherever you look, as is bog myrtle, which in a place like this is a bonus as a natural insect repellent.

There is an almost prehistoric feel to the open ruggedness of the land, powerful, as you stand and breathe in the cold fresh air. The last section of the path is buoyed by drums to keep it afloat, and we grab the railings to steady ourselves as we approach the steps ready to ascend the platform.

Luckily for us there is an enthusiastic and regular visitor to point out the osprey nest. Good job too, we'd never have found it without him, although when you know what to look for the silver stands of the cameras are evident. Across the moss to very black stump and then up at 10 o'clock to a short tree flattened on the top, there sits the nest. Not as high as you might have expected but giving a clear view all around.

Cetti's warbler is near the tower. I've rarely seen one, or seen what I think might be one, but the sound is unmistakable, possible the loudest warbler anywhere. There is one below me. And it's giving it some too. Stunning!

The cold, or impatience, gets the better of my wife and she leaves. She waves as she sees me looking. Shortly I follow and we head along to the main viewing platform, where fortunately for us the small crowd of people leave before we arrive. Well, we are in a pandemic, leaving the volunteer to us. Time to top up my knowledge of the slightly quirky osprey. They have a laptop connected to the cameras on ospreys' nest and it is awesome to get of view of the patient mother on the nest. She'll be there for a few weeks before she gets to leave for any time worth mentioning. Incubation is about five weeks. She's tolerant of the varying weather conditions too. This year is still very cold and extremely wet for May.

The juveniles will fledge at around seven weeks and the family will stay local whilst the youngsters learn to fly. The female will leave before they've learnt to hunt, and the male will get them started before he too leaves. When they figure they can hunt OK the youngsters will also leave. They all fly to Africa, via Spain, the youngsters, like most migrants find the way by themselves. An innate map?

The following year, only the adults will return. The juveniles will stay in Africa until old enough to reproduce, about 3 or 4 years old. The male will return to the same spot he brought up young last year, but the female will go further afield to find another male and another site thus keeping the gene pool varied and help strengthen a small population.

I learnt recently that apparently Osprey is lousy at successfully mating, so they need to have a lot of practice. Make of that what you will...

The female, as ever with birds of prey, is the larger of the species. And as the primary nest sitter probably needs to be as the nest can be prone to attack by many other birds such as corvids and other birds of prey including other ospreys. Size matters! The male becomes the provider of food, which in the case of Osprey is fish. As a result, Osprey nests, and obviously Ospreys are usually found near water, and water open enough to allow them to hunt.

Once a fish has been caught, the male will take it to a tree and eat most of the head and the meat and fatty tissue from the top or front of the fish. Whilst she's sitting the hen will then eat all that's left, adjusting her behaviour when the young hatch. They will be given the protein rich meat in the middle, and she will then content herself with the tail. It's funny though if you are ever lucky enough to see the male arriving at the nest with food it looks as though the female snatches the food from him. It is likely though that is the only way that she can get the food from him. Birds generally have three forward facing claws and one rear facing one. To accurately catch a fish Osprey rotates one talon to the rear and then cannot retract it once the fish is caught. The female has to rip the fish from the male to feed herself and her young.

Now that was a stunning example of how you can see fantastic examples of the wonder of our world just by being observant and interested. However, sometimes nature will present you with example of just how awesome our world is just when you need it, totally unbidden, and sometimes when you would least expect it.

The second time I saw Osprey, he was completely unexpected and unasked for, but utterly amazing, just by being himself.

It was a year or two after my trip to Russia and my wife and I were on a circumnavigation of the UK on holiday. At this time, we were in Dorset, somewhere near Studland Bay. The exact location and situation have been lost in the mists of time, but I do remember being at a fair of some kind, there were lots of people all around and for whatever reason I needed space as I'm sure you can empathise. I was feeling closed in, maybe just in my head, but maybe geographically as well. Sometimes I think we all do. I dragged my wife away from where ever we were, and we just drove. We drove along which ever road came our way and eventually we found a spot to pull in. We left the car and scrambled down a small bank. At least I did, my long-suffering wife a joined me a little later.

The fresh air was clearing my head, the sound of water lapping on the pebbles smoothed my soul and the sun was beginning to break through the clouds that dominated the sky. The waders that were there had evacuated when I arrived but were beginning to reappear. Redshank and Oystercatcher as I remember.

We may have been sat there a little while. I am able to be still and at peace in the countryside for quite a while and often exhaust the patience of those I am with. As I recover my sense of calm a large bird glides overhead and I instinctively reach for my binoculars. Unconsciously I raise them to my eyes which haven't left the bird I'm watching. As I have taught many an observer at Dungeness, (I worked as a field teacher for ten years with the RSPB) if you keep looking at what you want to see when you raise your binoculars to your eyes, you will be looking at exactly the same thing, just multiplied and much bigger.

The bird, as I'm sure you are aware is Osprey, big and magnificent. A bird I'd not seen since I left Russia. This time though I was to experience more than just this bird flying overhead. At a quick glance you could mistake her for a large greater black backed gull, but I quickly realised that this was not the case. They are just different. I imagine the confusion comes from the Ospreys long wings, compared to a buzzard for example and the lighter colours when seen from below.

I feel adrenaline start to run through me as I realise this bird is hunting and not just in passage from A to B. Excitement builds, I could be in with the chance of watching Osprey hunt. Que many massive adjectives here. As I said before Osprey hunts for fish. This is expected in the gulls and terns we consider to be sea birds; the main difference is that these birds are equipped for water and don't get water logged when they get wet. This is not the case with Osprey. These birds can get waterlogged, and if they do, they are likely to drown. So, the matter of hunting must be very scientific. Catching dinner is not only necessary to avoid starvation, it's extremely precarious too. As well as not getting waterlogged, superb judgement is also required when selecting the fish to target. Too deep and the risk of getting waterlogged increases, but also the size of fish targeted. If you can't let go once you have caught your fish and cannot lift it clear of the water and away you are also in trouble. Attempting to catch a fish and missing it is also a huge waste of energy. True for all hunters, but I imagine of greater danger for Osprey and the way she hunts.

The strike, however, is spectacular. She will 'hover' at various heights to access the fish and all variables assessing the chances of success. Osprey then dives, wings closed headfirst towards the water, but enters feet and talons first, striking the fish hard and quickly before leaving the water quickly and vigorously, shaking hard to shed as much water as possible. The fish is held headfirst to make it as aerodynamic as possible, the feet usually one behind the other.

The whole process is over in seconds in a major splash fest, from her entry, grabbing the fish and leaving before she takes on enough water to stop her departure and the shimmying that then takes place.

Lazily, she then flies away to the other side of the inlet and the world then returns to the residual quiet of normality.

And me? I have forgotten whatever discontent I was feeling probably not much more than a minute before. Now I have a sense of exultation combined with a newly found inner peace. Nature can do that for you. Mother Earth knows exactly when and where her gifts are best given.

Chapter 14.

The search for church (part two).

So, on our return from Italy I enthusiastically took up the search, that unfortunately, inevitably became a challenge to continue to find places that encourage the spirituality, peace and contemplation that we had found in Italy.

Unfortunately, England is not Italy (fortunately too). I must admit I have not investigated any Catholic Churches, as the cathedrals in Italy all were, but investigated Church of England churches.

The obvious first stop was our local church in Mongeham, and as was to become typical, it was locked. Which is a shame, many churches, we are led to believe, have been vandalised or had their sacred objects, crosses etc. stolen, so it is perhaps understandable that many churches, ours included, is accessed by getting a key from a local household. I, and many others I suspect would find this a barrier to entry, often we want to pop in when we have a moment, or even remember with short notice. Your first thoughts must be for those who have lost so much that they see no value in these artefacts, whether religious or spiritual; that they have no value other than financial. But then there will always be those who feel they have right to take whatever they feel they need. We have to see passed these signs of our times. The greatest inner peace cannot be found in money alone.

A search on google will yield interesting results too, the pervading will amongst those that govern and insure churches, the National Churches Trust, the Churches Conservation Trust or Ecclesiastical Insurance all encourage those responsible for the upkeep and welfare of churches to keep them open. Often these decisions are taken at a parish level.

You then wonder at the mentality that pervades, is it the fear that breeds in all our lives if we let it. Fear that someone will damage the church, or steal the important artefacts vital to religion, or the church. This not the place for a long debate into the issue, but surely the context here is that the churches should be open and open for everybody. A church has an ambience that is unique and whilst it is similar to our outdoors and possibly fulfils the same need, we shouldn't be restricted as to when we can fulfil it. It is easy to have preconceived notions of what may happen if we leave our churches open, especially if one church has suffered at the hands of those who do not value what is around them. Surely it would make more sense to have the church open and available to the community; even look for reasons to bring the community into the church and thus reduce the possibility of so-called undesirables doing what they do. We have to have faith in people, that the majority do and will continue to make the right choices. Maybe keep the artefacts of value in a safe place, for use at the appropriate time and put out wooden versions that have the same spiritual value, but less appeal to those whose intent is malign.

It was whilst walking the Ridgeway with my son that an open church was the most welcome site. It was raining, and raining down in sheets, as it had been all day. We had wet weather gear, good gear too, so we were prepared for whatever the weather might throw at us. We are experienced walkers, so were well prepared. That doesn't stop us from wanting to have a few moments out of the rain, as I have often said being outside is life enhancing, but so is the return to indoors.

There had been a sign outside the church offering shelter and also saying that tea, coffee and cake were available, so with a look and a nod, in we went. It was great to be able to shed our waterproofs, with their hoods and sealable cuffs, I hate hoods, when you look right or left all you see is the inside of the hood. We also took off our boots, there was no one else there to complain.

The Church of the Holy Trinity in Nuffield was a real blessing in itself, and just as all things appear, it appeared just when we needed it to.

We found the kettle, mugs and plates and the cake, yes there was cake, biscuits too, as promised. The church was a haven. There was an honesty box richly deserving of topping up. Someone here was a saint. And what better way, after it's intended purpose, for a church, is to serve not only it's local community, but even the wider one, than to provide shelter and refreshment. But then wasn't that one of the intentions for a church during their original inception?

Here was a service to the community that should stand as an example to the whole world. One that for us, was another coincidence, and as I've said before, there's too many of them, that proves that the law of attraction is real. It was there, just when we needed it.

And so back to Mongeham Church. It was shortly after my failed visit that I met up with the retired clergyman, who still lives in the village. The conversation was unexpected in content, I asked him how I might gain access to the church when there were no services on. His reply was based on any activities the church had on to involve the community and would be open, the flower show for example. He actually, didn't, expect me, to want to go and just spend some time in the church in contemplation, or meditation or whatever. Maybe the previous statement about preconceptions had another example right here.

Mongeham Church sits on top of Church Hill, to the northwest edge of the village and is, to me at least, as Kentish a church as a church can be. It is constructed of lime mortar and flints, and flints as we know are in large supply in this area of the country and the roof is constructed of red kent peg tiles. The tower is square, with a round turret on one corner that stands up above the rest of the tower. Typically for a village church there is a churchyard around it, beyond that a large building that is no longer the rectory and a sheep field that caused my dog to believe that sheep can bite from a distance. She didn't know what an electric fence was, obviously! But she stayed clear of sheep ever after.

I know that bats still roost in the rafters due to an enjoyable evening learning about bats was conducted within the church itself before going to look for bats in the churchyard at dusk with a bat detector, (in case we couldn't actually see any). The vicar told us how infuriating it was because they would poo on his bible which sat on the lectern. I think he just liked the story, because bat poo is dry and therefore easily dispersed and anyway, he could easily either move the bible or cover it up with a suitable plastic sheet. I think most of us would love to have bats roosting in our lofts. An honour.

But for me there is a much more interesting anecdote. One of the plaques on the wall to the top of this 13th century church is to a Captain Robert Maynard. He is credited with being one of Queen Elizabeth' the firsts privateers, as well as a sailor of note in the royal navy. I had some clients who lived locally, the husband had been a very prominent film director in the past. He had been looking to direct a film about Blackbeard the notorious pirate we have heard about in many a tale of dastardly behaviour befitting a pirate. Allegedly Johnny Depp was interested in the project. Said gentleman had been carrying out a lot of research and suspected that Captain Maynard may well have been that dastardly pirate. It was whilst researching the church for this very chapter that contrasting information has come to light that suggests that Captain Robert Maynard captured Blackbeard so therefore could not actually be him.

Fascinating, but once again I am off task.

At the top of the hill to the east of the village is Shoulden Church. Slightly simpler in construction than Mongeham and without the turret section to its tower it fairly neatly fits into the same description. On attempting to gain entry I discovered that the church is open to visitors between twelve and two pm every Friday. That's cool I thought, and despite holding that vital piece of knowledge, do you know how often I have managed to go in. Never, that's right, never. The number of times I have remembered at 2.30, the day before, even the morning before is huge. I have remembered that its open during these times on occasion, but never been in the locality when I have. Any comments about the law of attraction I made above are irrelevant here, this is SODS or Murphys Law depending on where you live.

However, across the path from Sholden Church is a kind of Sholden Church Graveyard Annexe.

It's one of those places that although you know it's there you never notice or think about it. A place that's kind of lost in space and time. It could've featured in Harry Potter like 12 Grimmauld Place. I have walked passed it, cycled passed it, driven passed it more times than I could possibly remember. I even noticed that the walls had been knocked down but didn't really notice it was there until one day I saw that the gate was open. It was like an invitation, when I got a moment, I would go in. And funnily enough unlike the church itself one day I did actually go in.

There are places in this world where time seems to stop, when you enter the world seems to become a faraway place. Road noise seems to fade into the distance, as does the sounds of walkers, chatting as they call their dogs in as they meet the road. Where the sounds of hedge trimmers lower to a mesmeric hum and the outside world seems to almost cease to exist, almost as if you are entering the faerie realm. Except that for the animal world nothing had changed at all. Blackbirds still look for worms, and robins still guard territories as if their entire existence depends upon it. Insect buzz, hoverflies hover and bees struggle against their increasing payload of pollen and seem to know that our existence depends upon them. And if I could see them mice would forage and seek successfully to avoid detection so as to continue their existence.

It was into this almost conscience altering graveyard that I entered one summers evening. Gillian my wife had gone to the theatre with a friend, and I determined I would be my time to go. When I finished my chores for the day, I cycled up the hill and entered the churchyard, almost cautiously, as if, as I was entering somewhere uncharted. There have not been any burials here for a long time, but somebody obviously came from time to time, the grass was strimmed and the path had been cleared. Looking around me and taking in the altered state of my surroundings, well as I perceived them, I wandered carefully to the end of the path, carefully propped up my bike and found a place to sit. Somewhere free of brambles and stinging nettles.

And I meditated, let my thoughts drift away, acknowledged any that were persistent, but kept letting them go. Listened carefully to the sounds that were around me, let any smells that were there reach my stillness, and stimulate my subconscious mind. Often when I meditate, I have a predetermined time to finish, and it's amazing how you can set a mental alarm clock when you meditate that's almost as accurate as a clock. But here I just sat for however long was necessary. I was there for an hour or two. Maybe it's experiences like these that conjured up the notion of getting lost in the world of the Fey, where those that thought they were there for minutes were lost for days, or years, or decades. In the same way that maybe damselflies led to the possibilities of fairies. And maybe children can see them because they believe.

When I left, however much later, I certainly had a sense of peace that is sometimes hard to find.

What's most important though is that these places exist all over towns and cities, we just need to go and look for them.

The next instalment in the 'search for church' occurred on a Thursday morning, I had been networking and had a meeting with a lady I had met at the Kent Wedding Circle, I was still looking for people to work with who could help me get an event up and running. We had arranged to meet in 'Mama Feelgoods' in Bekesbourne at 11 that day, that meant that I had an hour or so to fill.

Perfect time to see if St. Peters Church in Bekesbourne would be open. Following the signs from the road you follow a little track alongside a small stream and leave your car there. You then walk up a path to the church that sits on the hillside just to the side of the village. It looks similar in design and size and structure to Sholden Church that I mentioned above. As you can imagine it is locked, 'due to its remote location'. The key is available locally, but again the time it would take to get the key, enjoy a visit, and then return it makes the whole task prohibitive. Fortunately, there are a number of benches in the surrounding graveyard. I went and sat on one at the edge and had a very peaceful half hour until one of the locals came and we spent several minutes chatting. Her husband and son are buried in the churchyard, and she likes to keep their graves cared for and tidy. She is largely alone in Bekesbourne, her grandchildren are in London. Lovely to pass the time.

She also mentioned that she thought Patrixbourne church was open just a short walk way. It would've taken about twenty minutes to walk and again a similar time should I have returned to my car and gone that way, so again, not possible at that moment either. Churchyards it has to be said were locations I was becoming familiar with.

Funnily enough it was the churchyard that I had been most familiar with growing up that actually yielded success. As a teenager I had mown the lawns at The Church in Worth dedicated to St. Peter and St. Paul. It was a summer Saturday job that I wasn't overly enthusiastic about, but my Dad had got me the job and as a teenager the money was pretty handy. I had a girlfriend at the time, and she used to come and keep me company and as you can imagine, that helped. The biggest difficulty was the small square shaped 'headstones' when the grass was really growing at its fastest, it was hard to find the time to mow the churchyard regularly enough to stop them vanishing into the grass. And then they would catch the mower unexpectedly and prang the mower blades. Even though there was a strimmer available, I didn't think the job through well enough as a teenager to remember to strim around these little gravestones first.

It is also the churchyard that houses the ashes of both my parents, my father from 2007 and later my mother in 2015. My attendances to visit them are erratic to say the least. Rarely on birthdays or Christmas, but when I'm going passed the end of the road and I think about it. I do think of them with a fair amount of regularity, my father when I 'flick' the woodcutter in the music room at home, just after I wind the grandfather clock. My Grandmother too.

It would have been on one of these visits that I saw the sign outside that actually said 'open to visitors' it had probably been there all the time, but as usual we often only see things when we are looking, or are meant to see them... After paying my respects in I went, the last time I would have gone inside Worth Church would've been for my sister's wedding nearly 30 years ago.

Worth Church has a spire sitting proudly above flint walls and above the entrance way containing two large oak doors.

The ashes are to the south of the church by a magnificent yew. These are some of the most amazing trees, commonly found in churchyards, probably because they are long lived and churchyards tend to stay dedicated to their purpose for long periods too.

Inside the church I sat for 10 to 20 minutes on a pew and just enjoyed the peace, the ambience, the stillness so necessary in this busy world. And then I went on a gentle wander around the church and took in the windows. The meaning of most of them is lost on me, but the artwork and the sheer majesty of them is not, nor the effect that they have on the light in a church or the effect that has on the mind, whether real or perceived. Also, the wall plaques dedicated to the Hendersons of Felderland.

John Henderson, a prominent Naval Purser used his 'prize' money for captured enemy ships to buy two farms in the early 1800's, one of which was Felderland. The land passed to his son William, a successful farmer, justice of the peace and Church Warden for the Parish of Worth, then known as Word, and the source of the phrase 'Word in Worth' which can be seen around the village.

I took in the columns, the skilfully carved lectern and masoned columns. I wandered around the organ and looked to see where the access to the steeple light be. Fonts are always ornate, what they represent to churchgoers is huge. As is any symbolism in any religion.

And whilst I will never stop looking for open churches when the opportunity presents itself, I haven't found any more. I have been back to Worth Church several times, comfortable in the knowledge that it's open.

And, again, there are two other interesting points of note here. All this when I don't actually consider myself a Christian, but maybe it's because churches have tended to be built on religious sites of other faiths, to impose the new beliefs upon whatever the religion originally served. Usually to serve an ego, or possibly misguided good intent whatever, but specialness is never lost...

I guess ultimately my church is where I can feel the sun and the wind and the rain on my face. Where I have space to be and celebrate and breathe. And space to heal my hurts.

Space to be me.

Chapter 15.

Unlocking the WEB. The 4 keys.

Introduction

The world is in crisis. NO IT REALLY IS! And the signs are everywhere.
Maybe you need to be of a certain age to see them, and even then you
actually need to be looking. Looking and remembering too, hence
certain age.

All of the creatures we share our lives with are suffering population
losses at unprecedented levels. This is not the place for an in-depth
scientific analysis, but any of us of a certain age will have noticed that
there are far fewer sparrows for example than there used to be. As a
child they were everywhere, all the time. Now, if you look around the
flocks are fewer in number and the number of birds in a totally wild
flock is in the region of 10 – 12, if not fewer. Even the number of
swallows zooming around our skies like marauding 'topguns' seem to be
in short supply.

Summers were often dominated by large numbers of hover flies that
would take up a space just in front of your face, unthreateningly I might
add, before flitting away to do the same in another location a small
distance away. And getting replaced by another one. Those calm
summer glades were full of them.

Butterflies were everywhere, hedgerows and meadows in summer were full of them. Red admirals and peacocks, gatekeepers and meadow browns to name a few, or even 'cabbage whites' so called, were abundant everywhere, so much so that we didn't even notice them.

The list of insect species that were everywhere is almost endless, woodlouse, earwigs, mosquitos even, endless different kinds of beetles. Stag beetles, standing proud, with those great big antlers the males have, harmless but very impressive. There was a time when I'd return home on my motorbike in summer and the front of it and the front of my helmet would be black with insect corpses, not any more...

And the number of cuckoos we hear now has fallen away dramatically. Each spring would be spent waiting for the first one to call. Now I often get to mid-summer before I think, I haven't heard a cuckoo yet!

And the news has reported on the decline of the humble bumblebee with increasing regularity. The length of time we have if bumblebees leave the earth varies depending on the report we hear. But however long we have, its within a human lifespan, so why aren't we all actively looking to do something to prevent that catastrophe?

Probably because of that human response to so many conditions, 'it can't happen to me!' or the mentality that just see's nature as a resource for making money. How long do we have to wait before we stop those lines of thought?

Now it is at this point that I have to stop. I can hear my wife telling me, 'you've got to stop preaching to people, they don't want to hear it.' And of course there's another rant right there. But this is about solutions, not problems. You have bought this book because you want to know, so of course I'm preaching to the converted.

The solution.

So, where do we start?

Well like any plan, we start with the 'big' goal, what we ultimately want, which on its own is impossible; in this case a world full of all the life that was accidentally or intentionally, (you decide) put here, and evolved to live with everything else that is, or, is still meant to be, on this planet and then we break that goal into smaller and smaller tasks until we get to tasks that we can actually make a start on. Thus, we start small, and we start at the beginning and we build up a massive butterfly effect, whilst never losing sight of our ultimate goal. So, we start in our own backyard. And that cliché is particularly relevant because if we add together all our backyards, or gardens, and make them into fantastic wildlife friendly areas we will have more total wildlife friendly spaces than we currently have, than if we add together all the nature reserves and national parks. Certainly in this country, but if we expand that thought across the globe, then probably there too.

All we need then is a little knowledge and a little desire, and a little understanding of the way the world works. The initial benefits would be huge on their own, a better place for everything to live, with more variety, more wonder, more life, but if you turn that around, more life, more wonder and more variety in our own lives. And when you think about that, why wouldn't you want it? A better place to live in and a life filled with wonder.

We do not need to be experts to make a difference, we just need a basic understanding of the way the natural world works. A favourite phrase of mine is that, ' I know more than most and less than many.' And that is more than enough. A fantastic place to start is what I call, 'the 4 keys'.

The 4 KEYS

A lot of our wildlife can find its way into our gardens unaided, but with a little thought we can encourage a lot more. There are four things we can address which will increase the life we share our life with very simply and easily, and they are

- Access
- Shelter
- Food
- Water.

The first key then is.

Access

By access I mean not only access to our gardens, but also access to available shelter. Whilst many of the creatures we share our lives with can access our gardens easily, there are some that can't.

Hedgehog suffers greatly due to modern fencing.

Similarly, we insulate and seal up our lofts to stop heat escaping out into the atmosphere and make our houses more efficient insulators, thus reducing our bills and using less fuel to keep us warm. But bats have used our houses to roost in during the day and over winter for so long many have forgotten where they used to roost. Birds nest in our lofts and also in the eaves. Some species of bees do to.

There are ways of providing alternative access if we are aware of the issues and have a desire to solve them. We can cut four-inch holes in the kickboards of our fences, or make sure there is room enough under a gate. It is advisable to put a hedgehog hole on each expanse of fence to allow hedgehogs to roam more freely. They need 1–2 km to roam in a night. We need to avoid the 'drop in the ocean' reality if at all possible.

We can actually accommodate the needs of wildlife in the structure of our houses too. There are bricks that can be used that allow birds access to nest spaces and roof tiles that can also allow access to loft spaces that aren't too detrimental to our fuel bills. We can even assign spaces within our lofts to contain birds where we are happy for them to be and that will save them making an undesirable mess.

That brings us logically to the second Key.

Shelter

I don't think there's a creature on this earth that wants to be outside when the wind is howling and the rain is horizontal, so therefore the more homes we can provide specific to the creatures that will use them it follows that the more creatures we will have in our gardens. That ranges from nest boxes, to log piles and insect hotels or bat boxes. There's no guarantee that they will all be used, we don't buy every house we look at, we like a choice and many of the creatures we share our lives with are the same.

If we are creative when we plan our gardens it can be fairly simple to incorporate animal homes into the very fabric of our gardens. Hedgehog boxes or animal hotels under decking is one (or two?) examples.

The only certainty is that if we provide no homes, we will home nothing.

And what does everything like to do at home? They like to eat.

Food

The animal world doesn't have access to supermarkets. All creatures must eat enough food to survive the night, which in winter can be bitterly cold, even with some form of shelter. And then have enough energy to go and find food the next day. And remember, that food doesn't want to be caught and eaten.

So, as responsible hosts, it is our duty to put out suitable food. Birds will eat a range of differing foods from seeds to nuts and mealworms, or fruit or bacon rinds, all which have specific kinds of feeders to allow birds access, but not the range of creatures you don't want to attract. You need to see what works best for you. Also bear in mind that favourite foods may change between birds of the same species, they have preferences the same as we do.

A very important rule though is always put feeders where you can see them. If you're going to bring birds into your garden, make sure you get the maximum enjoyment out of them for yourself.

Food for many insects is actually the planting you have included, bees for example favour flowers in the purple spectrum, perennial wallflower, hebes or salvias or foxgloves to name a few.

It's worth noting here that all of the 'single' types of flower are the best ones to plant. Single flowers are the one that have a basic design, like daffodils, or foxgloves for example and haven't been altered by geneticists to pander to the preferences of an often ill informed buying public. Single flowers have all their reproductive parts intact as nature intended and can be pollinated by insects, thus carrying out the purpose that nature intended. We need all the pollination we can possibly get. Often the clue to which plants have been altered is in the name, often those altered are often called double. These flowers have no scent either.

So, it thus makes sense to leave as many flowers as possible in their natural habitat rather than pick them and take them indoors. Or make sure we grow enough to justify our pleasures.

Let's plant food that is food rather than something that just looks pretty, which as a by-product will often have a great scent that we can enjoy as well as the insects it was designed to attract. Jasmine or honeysuckle spring to mind.

And with food, most of us like to drink, one way or another.

Water

Everything needs to drink. Some creatures will get all the water they need from what they eat, some drink very little and some a lot.

But water for many creatures is more than just something to drink. It's home for a part or all of their lives. So its shelter for them.

And that is why every wildlife friendly garden should include a pond.

A pond is the greatest single source of wonder you can include in your garden. A huge variety of life, some of which is often the most beautiful, constructed wonderfully by mother nature, with the most breath-taking designs this world has to offer; are housed in this medium which also houses large parts of the food webs we are trying to encourage and install into our gardens and lives.

So, Food Webs

In effect then the 4 keys actually help us to install as many involved and intricate food webs into our gardens as possible. It makes sense then to briefly describe what a food web is. You might remember the phrase from school days, words you had to pay lip service to, to pass an exam or get a good grade in an essay. But in reality, they are one of the most important systems this world hosts to keep us all alive. Put simply, a food web describes the flow of energy from the sun to that eco systems top predator, as well as all the different systems that are contained within that, hence the term food web rather than food chain. Albeit food webs are actually constructed of various food chains all of which are intricately linked.

To understand a food web, it's probably simplest to look at a few simple food chains. All energy comes from and therefore begins flowing from the sun, plants can transform this heat and light energy into food energy during a process called photosynthesis. They take in carbon dioxide and release oxygen. Herbivores then eat plants and herbivores are eaten by carnivores. So a simple chain might be sun, grass, snail, small bird, large bird, or sun, algae, pond snail, dragonfly nymph, fish, bird. And then of course another food chain gets set up when any creature dies, they will be consumed by scavengers that might be vultures or buzzards or crows, what is left will then begin to rot and decay and is broken up further by detritivores such as the various beetles assigned the task, until everything is absorbed back into the earth thus providing nutrients for various plants to grow and harvest energy from the sun and it all begins again. There are numerous chains and ultimately when they combine you then begin to get the numerous webs that make up and contain life. Amazing and mind boggling really.

However, despite how amazing the food webs are, many of the creatures we share our lives with have a life that is so utterly fantastic in what they are and what they can do, that when we really think about it we have to just go WOW because with all the technology at our disposal we still can't do what they can do, housed within a body of their size.

A world full of Awe.

Here we are going to look at some of the creatures in our world, celebrating them for what they are and how by unlocking each of the four keys for them we can bring them into our lives, which we then enhance by their presence and by increasing their numbers and thus prolong the future of our world and thus provide a future for our children too.

Bumblebee

The bumblebee is a natural wonder, period. Firstly, because there is probably no more important a creature on this planet. And that is no idle passing comment, because this insect singlehandedly keeps every other creature on this planet alive. Genuinely!!! And that is because it pollenates everything that either we eat, or everything we eat, eats. There are other pollinators out there, but the bumble bee does the lion's share of the work.

Maybe it's at this point that I should briefly explain pollination. A bee whilst collecting nectar and pollen will brush up against the stamen (male part) of a flower and collect pollen as she goes, take it to the stigma (female part) and deposit some of it there. Or to the female part of another plant. The flower can then grow new seeds and thus new flowers. The bumblebee does all this unintentionally whilst going about its own business of collecting nectar. Rather altruistic really. It's for this reason that I struggle to see why there aren't more people and business' trying really hard, totally intentionally, to plant as many plants popular with the many species of bee we live with as is possible. No brainer really...

Plants such as lavender, jasmine, hebe, buddleia, lafateria, perennial wallflower, honesty and bluebells to name a few. They make our world colourful and wonderfully aromatic, as well as giving us the spectacle of bees in our gardens.

Secondly, bees are spectacular in their own right. The cliché 'if bees can fly then ....' With whatever chosen ending is there for whatever inspiring reason it is used. The fact that bees can fly at all given their size and the size of their wings is little short of miraculous. Think about for a minute, they have a pretty big body, and some of them are massive, the big female of the buff tailed bumble bee is one of our biggest and the first to emerge in spring, she's about 2cm in length. Now think about her size and then look at her tiny little wings, even though she has four of them they have to go like the clappers to keep her airborne. You can feel the air vibrating at anything up to a meter, or so, away as she goes past. You'll often actually hear them coming before you see them.

So the fact that she can fly at all is very impressive, but then the purpose of her flight is to collects pollen and nectar. We have already established she's quite heavy already, she then loads herself up with pollen and nectar and still has to fly back to the nest. Even more WOW than before. Very impressive. It's for this reason we often see bees grounded on a path or on our lawns. It's because they are exhausted. And she has still got to get back to the colony.

Only a newly fertilised queen will over winter, all other females, including the old queen and males will die at the end of the summer. In spring the queen will find a new nest, lay and feed a few eggs, all by herself at first! When these hatch, the new workers will take over all duties and the queen will stay in the nest until the cycle repeats.

There are 18 species of bee in this country, the most common are the buff tailed, mentioned above, but also the white tailed, or the red tailed, all traditional barred and the carder bee much more buff and orange. Have a look next time you see, or hear one, as it goes passed.

So, as we already share our lives with bees, what can we do to help them? That's where the four keys come into play.

The 4 Keys

Access

Access is pretty easy for bees; they can fly through or over most of our boundaries.

Shelter

But homes we can give significant help with. Although not as large an honeybee populations, bumblebees are still social insects often living in underground colonies, under sheds or in holes in the ground, any unused hole will do. They like to have existing nesting material in the box so like used bird boxes, but purpose-built boxes will also be used if they have a small hole, approximately 2cm in diameter, and a couple of ventilation holes. Make sure the box is in a shaded spot and near nectar rich flowers. You will need more than one box though because they will only use it once. Clean them out and change their location.

Food and Water

Bumblebees eat pollen and drink nectar and that's it, so for food and drink it's all about the planting. The plants listed above are good examples to plant and there are many mentioned in literature and on the internet. The list is long, but one great way to buy plants specifically for bees is to go to the garden centre and look to see which plants the bees are all over. Buy them.

Bat

Have you ever watched a bat flying? Totally unlike a bird, but then they are not birds, and not like an insect either. Rapid direction changes are the norm, possibly due to the sounds received from their echo location system for finding their way about and finding their food.

In the hot summer months, they can be seen flitting over our hedgerows in the countryside at dusk as they hunt for the insects that make up their food supply. Dusk because they are nocturnal creatures and get up as we should be going to bed. I assume they are nocturnal because as hunters they are not as good as daylight hunters and would be out competed. As predators they pretty much have the skies to themselves at night, indeed owls, our other nocturnal specialists are after different prey.

And watching them on a summers evening from the comfort of your own favourite chair in your own garden is a joy. When they are about there is a real sense of awe and excitement. when they grace your garden with their presence before vanishing just as unexpectedly as they arrived, they leave you with a sense of wonder and privilege.

So, as hunters they have two outstanding points of note, firstly, they are the only mammal that can fly. Yes, bats are mammals, they have vertebra, are covered in fur, give birth to live young that the female suckles, everything else in the air is a bird or an insect. This means that the bats wing has to be a development of the mammalian arm and pentadactyl limb, or hand. Which is a pretty awesome feat of evolution. The upper arm and fore arm form a shallow v and the fingers radiate away from the wrist to give support to the skin that stretches across them and reaches almost down to the ankles to form a wing. Totally un-bird like, or insect like for that matter. Which I imagine is why their flight is totally 'bat' like I guess. Can you imagine the strength needed to lift yourself into the air and then stay aloft by muscle power alone, especially when most of the 'weight' is borne by your long fingers...?

But then comes the real awesome wow bit, the way they get about... and the first thing we must get our head around is that bats are actually not blind, their sight is of a similar level to ours, believe it or not. But with that in mind you can see why they need a better way of getting about if they are out at night time. They don't need street lights or come to that any kind of light.

Where they really differ from us sensually is in their hearing, which really is super sensitive. And it needs to be to hear the variations in sound made by the echoes that come from the kind of 'shouting' that they do repeatedly. Some children can hear their calls, but for most of us they are beyond our range of hearing, although you can now buy bat detectors that will make their chatter audible for the narrow range of frequencies we can hear. These sounds are reflected by everything they hit. What is really amazing though, is that the bat can work out so much from these echoes. Anything out there that is solid and needs to be avoided, as well as things that are moving and also need to be avoided in case they are a predator, and most importantly, things that are moving and can be eaten. This is called echo location and the more you get your head around it the more amazing it becomes. Just shut your eyes and imagine you have to repeatedly make sounds and then interpret them to find your way about and catch food. How long would you last? And that is in the dark whilst flying. Unreal.

Bats are small and so their metabolic rate is very high, as a result they need a lot of food and adults will catch insects in their thousands during a single night.

Another wonder of nature.

And so we should also include a little bit of natural history so that we have a little bit of understanding of these amazing little creatures.

Another feature of bat life is hibernation, and whilst normal for a bat, it's almost impossible to really imagine as a human, however much at times we may wish that we could do it. The speed of all their body functions drops to the minimum required to stay alive, they enter a state called torpor. Hibernation begins in November, although ambient temperature and food supply may delay or advance the need. They will spend increasingly longer periods asleep until they just don't wake up and typically stay asleep until at least February when exceptionally hungry they may wake on warmer nights and go in search of food.

By the time May arrives they are fully active and will go in search of nursery sites, giving birth to a single pup in June. The pups feed on mother's milk until august when they will begin flying and start taking real food, they do not have long before they will have the skill to catch enough food to build up their fats for the winter.

Adults will then begin courtship rituals; roosts will become more mating sites than maternally based and sexual activity increases as does the need to build up fat reserves for winter. As temperatures begin to cool down then longer stages of torpor become prevalent.

The 4 keys.

Access

As with bumblebees' access is not a problem.

Shelter

However, a place to safely roost is becoming more of an issue. Traditionally bats roost in caves, but as humans began to settle and began building bigger and more expansive dwellings, they began using the available roof space as a safe and suitable roosting place. Even better when we began putting ceilings into our rooms and the roof spaces became undisturbed roosts.

Whilst churches are still popular places for roosting, our homes are becoming less and less so. We seal them up and lag them so as not to heat the night sky and spend less on our fuel bills. Great for us but not so good for bats.

Luckily though you can buy bat boxes. They are easily told apart from bird boxes by the way they are entered. The entrance is on the bottom. The wood is ridged so that a bat can land on it and then scramble up into the roosting cavity. The boxes should be placed in a quiet location at least 5m high and facing south with clear access to allow the bat to fly into it unobstructed.

<u>Food and Water</u>

As bats like to catch their food on the wing there is not much to be done about providing food, although you could try putting out mealworms. Bats skim water and take a drink on the way passed it. Sounds have a mostly unique echo from water because it is flat. So although they have to drink, they need a large expanse of it to know it's there. Food and drink then, difficult for us to provide for bats, but not impossible.

Hedgehog

My first knowledge of hedgehogs was my Aunt reading me stories of Mrs Tiggywinkle, Beatrix Potter's home loving, house cleaning and cooking hedgehog. I didn't think much more about them until a few years ago when I read about them on Facebook, and how their numbers were falling at an alarming rate. They didn't appear in any of my studies when I was at college and I suppose a little like sparrows, they were just a creature that was a part of the countryside and had been and always would be there. Except that just like sparrows, their numbers were falling too. It's just that they didn't have an organisation as big as the RSPB (Royal Society for the Protection of Birds) to shout as loudly for them as the sparrow did.

With just a little knowledge of their biology and ecology I would speak about them when networking and do the little I could to raise their plight and inform people of their status and give some suggestions as to how we could help these charming and secretive creatures in their hunt for food and shelter and thus help to increase their numbers. After all these are creatures that live in our gardens and our countryside and just should be there.

I dutifully joined the Hedgehog Preservation Society and arranged a meeting with the local 'hedgehog' lady who lived just off the town centre. It was amazing to get up close and personal with a real live hedgehog, although as the lady said. 'You'll only ever find a sick hedgehog out, or even awake, during the day', and so the hedgehog I met was in exactly the right place. Half its spines were missing, and mange was clearly in evidence. She had many other guests that were thankfully asleep and a few that were due to be released back to the wild shortly thereafter.

Another fact that was quite astonishing was that she had many hedgehogs that visited at night which was cool in itself, but not as amazing as the fact that they were not the hedgehogs she'd released, they were ones that had found her place and kept returning, and whilst that was awesome what was even more awesome was that actually getting to her garden was a feat in itself. She had made sure that there were hedgehog holes in her gates, which was sensible, but there were three of them and about 40m of paths to pass through to get to her garden, and of course the same path on the way out. Some of us have an affinity for certain animals and hedgehog certainly had an affinity for her.

She also showed me her hedgehog boxes, which as a garden designer and landscaper I loved. She had adapted garden benches to double up as hedgehog houses. A superb way of dual purposing a garden feature and one I look to incorporate with my work where ever possible.

Hedgehogs are unique in our garden landscapes, we like to think of them as quintessentially English, but there are eighteen different species worldwide and the European hedgehog (our version) has a population that spreads throughout Europe. They can live just about anywhere in the British Isles just as long as they've got food and shelter. And shelter is very important for them because they are one of a very select group of British creatures that truly hibernate. They do exactly what bats do, and as I have described the process in great detail above, I won't go through it again here.

The most significant visual feature of a hedgehog has to be the spines, made of keratin just like human hair, there are approximately 6000 of them per hedgehog and they are roughly 3cm in length. A hedgehog's skin covers it loosely so for most of the time and the spines lay flat, but when the hedgehog feels threatened it rolls into a ball, pulls its skin tight, a bit like one of those shopping bags and becomes a tight ball that is hard to penetrate.

Unless you are a badger. The badger is the main predator for a hedgehog and one of the main reason hedgehog numbers have fallen. You see badger has protected status, and when it was put in place it was rightly so, badger numbers were low. As a result, their numbers have increased. Which is definitely a good thing, as with hedgehogs, badgers are a creature that just should be in our countryside, but their numbers are now large enough to have an impact on hedgehogs and due to their protected status, they cannot be controlled.

Hedgehogs will begin waking up in March April time. Initially the search for food will occupy them until the need for procreation will begin to preoccupy them. The 'rut' can be a noisy affair, initially one male trying to impress a female with snorts, grunts and circular motions. Often these do little more than attract other males and the ruckus can be quite loud. As you can imagine mating has to be carefully enacted with all those spines to negotiate. Eventually the female will make her choice and she'll gestate for 30 – 40 days giving birth in June July time to 3 – 5 hoglets. Often only 2 – 3 will usually survive. They head out on their own about 10 days later. In very good years the female may raise a second brood, but they will have little time to fatten up enough to survive the winter.

Primarily carnivorous hedgehogs will eat any bugs, slugs, caterpillars, beetles etc they come across. Not a great fan of snails though, which is a shame, but they will remove many of the unwanted garden residents making the discerning gardener a happy fellow.

Eventually the need to hibernate will dominate a hedgehogs thoughts in October or November and they will go looking for a home for the winter.

The 4 keys.

Access

Access is a major issue for a hedgehog and one of the reasons that hedgehog number have been in decline. This issue though can simply be addressed. So let us start at the beginning. As we search for ever better value for money, we look to spend our money as efficiently as possible. Back when I was still running a landscaping business we were often asked, 'what is the cheapest way to put up a fence?' Our answer was always, 'put it up once'. And that means concrete fence posts, concrete kick boards and feather edge panels. Our fences will last a long time, great for us, but rubbish for hedgehogs. To them they are an impenetrable barrier that cannot be breached, and access to our gardens in the search for food is impossible.

A hedgehog can have a territory of 10 – 20 hectares and roam up to 2 km a night hunting for food, so access to all our gardens makes foraging a much simpler process and reduces the size of territory required.

Putting a 10cm square hole in a kick board or the bottom of a gate can make a huge difference, but put one on every side of your garden, otherwise your lone hole is just a drop in the ocean. And talk to your neighbours so that then you can set up a network of gardens for your local hedgehogs, after all, the more food there is available, the more likely you are to have a hedgehog once they have found your little hedgehog oasis.

Shelter

Whilst on the subject of 10cm holes, make sure any hedgehog box you make or buy has an entrance of this size. We have bought many that we have had to enlarge with a jigsaw. Hedgehog boxes can be bought or made and vary in style as much as your imagination will allow. Below ground, above ground, underneath decking, part of a garden bench, the possibilities are endless. They can be made of wood, netting, plastic, whatever, just leave materials for nesting available and the hedgehog will do the rest. An entrance chamber with a second door is ideal, or if the box will be underground, make sure the access tunnel is accessible all the way in. Leave some food near the entrance to make this home even more appealing. Just install your hedgehogs new home in a quiet undisturbed spot, and avoid it facing north or east and it'll be good to go.

Hedgehog will use homes during the day in summer and then continue to use them for hibernation, so put them out as soon as you can and wait. Often a sign that they are in residence, as well as flattened ground is a pathway to the entrance, often there will be scats left near the entrance a couple of cm in length and containing crushed shells of beetles for example.

Food and water

Food and drink, well any meat and water. Just not bread and milk, they can't digest bread properly and are lactose intolerant so milk will make them ill.

And from there, sit back, wait and enjoy.

House Martin

There is a romantic sentimental image I have of beautiful, thatched cottages with martin nests along the eaves, it is a sunny spring afternoon and house martins are flying in with food for their chicks. The arc they fly through as they arrive is perfect, as is the one when they leave. Very fairy-tale, and lovely.

Easily recognised from their relatives the swallow, they have deep blue upper parts with white undersides, the white extending to the topside at the base of the tail. Which is distinguished from the swallows distinct fork by just indenting in the centre. And their other close cousin the sand martin which is brown.

There used to be martin nests on the house next-door when we first moved in, but they got removed, unwisely I might add, when the house got redecorated. Needless to say, the martins have never returned.

That has never stopped me looking for martin nests and the wonderful flight of the inhabitants whenever I walk through villages or smaller towns.

In fact, it's the flight, or rather the journeys that these little birds undertake in migration each year that really makes them stand out with a huge WOW factor amongst those creatures we share our homes and gardens with.

We begin to look out for them during April or May, eagerly awaiting their arrival back from Southern Africa. And whilst the journey in itself is amazing, what is more amazing is the fact that they know the way from the minute they leave the egg, or maybe even before. You see the birds you see flying around in September are the youngsters, the adults will have left in August their parental duties over. The juveniles leave a little later and must find the way all by themselves.

That journey at an age of maybe 4 months is nothing short of spectacular. They have to cross the English Channel; water provides no 'lift' like they would get flying over hills and mountains on land. They then have to fly over France, and the French are prone to shooting everything, then cross the Mediterranean, which is larger than the English Channel. Cross the Deserts of North Africa, including the Sahara and keep going until they find their wintering roosts. The danger here is enhanced by the fact that a lot of the southern tribesmen consider them to be a delicacy and catch them as they go to roost in the evening.

And then as the temperatures cool in the southern hemisphere, they begin to make their way back to the north and the dangers they faced during their travel south.

Luckily for them, they feed on insects which are usually plentiful as they journey in either direction. If only we would be so lucky. Can you imagine if our offspring, at say age twenty, were faced with the instruction 'OK, we're off now, see you on the other side of the world in a month or so'. Daunting.

Typically, martins nest twice in a year, eggs are incubated for about a fortnight and the young fledge in approximately three weeks. They are fed for about a week after leaving the nest and then generally left to it although sometimes youngsters from the first brood will help feed the second.

The 4 Keys

Access

Access, for house martin, a master of flight, this is easy. In fact, unless there is a hobby doing the rounds, being airborne means access to anywhere is without danger for the most part.

Shelter

Martins generally nest in cup shaped nests under the eaves at the top of our houses. They may nest in the same nest year after year but will decorate afresh on each occasion. Although south east facing is typical, a common factor for nest location is the availability of soft mud for refurbishing the nest for a new season. Ready formed nests can be bought and put up, but make sure there is access to soft mud, then the nest is more likely to be used, Martins will want to decorate it to their own preferences. They are generally colonial so putting up two or three nests might also be an important consideration. Also, the access should be smaller than a sparrow, the martin will see to this, but sparrows are prone to taking over martin nests.

Food and drink

Food iscaught on the wing. Insects of any type that are small enough to catch. Generally, house martin hunts higher than swallow so avoids competition for the same prey. Unfortunately, not much the enthusiastic gardener can do to entice them in with food.

And unfortunately, you are unlikely to entice Martins to <u>drink</u> either.

Spider

It is amazing the reception that even the mention of spiders can bring. When I am out giving presentations there is a noticeable intake of breath from sections of any audience when they are mentioned. You have to wonder why? Fear of spiders is not an innate behaviour, we are only afraid of heights and loud noises when we are born, it's a learned behaviour. Most of those that are afraid of spiders have copied it from a parent or other trusted elder. You then have to ask where they learnt it and you may have to go back so far you have to look at the spider instead.

In this country there are (allegedly) no spiders with mouthparts big enough to penetrate our skin, so maybe the behaviour has been imported, or maybe it has been spread through entertainment media?

Or maybe it's due to the way that spiders move. After all they have eight legs, that might be it, but insects have six and none of them (not even wasps) generate the reaction that spiders do.

It is worth noting here that even with the major advances we have made with technology in the last few decades we still cannot make anything that can move with eight legs like a spider or as fast. It is possible that that's because we have no need, but it just makes the spider an even more amazing example of natural biological engineering. Not only can it control eight multi jointed legs in just the right order to move, but move really fast, and some of them can run incredibly fast, their livelihood is dependent on it, but also jump (some species) incredibly high. What was the selective pressure that favoured eight legs anyway?

So maybe it's a combination of all these factors. I don't suppose the movie, 'the Lord of the Rings' has helped either.

Love or hate them though, you have to be in awe of those that make webs surely. What an amazing ability! Just think about it for a minute, the majority of spiders are small, and yet these small creatures can make webs, and they make two different types of webbing too. If they were all sticky, they couldn't go and wrap up the unfortunate prey that's trapped in their web. The web that stretches out from the centre of the web to its external supports is not sticky. Especially handy when these are the first constructs of the web. Another WOW is that when these strands are complete the spider can change the composition of the web so that the ever-expanding circles are sticky. Amazing. Web is made or extruded from spinnarets.

An interesting thought then follows. What is the energy pay off? Making a web must be exhausting. How many flies must be consumed to make one web? Especially important when you consider that some spiders only feed once a month. Something to ponder the next time you brush one aside.

Another amazing thing about webs is the way that baby spiders disperse. They just let out a strand of web until it is long enough for the wind to take the optimistic baby aloft and carry it to an unknown destination.

On the subject of baby spiders, another quirk of spider biology, the male is much smaller than the female and risks his life every time the need or opportunity for a sexual encounter presents. Males if they are not quick, careful and strategic during a sexual encounter are very likely to get eaten. Generally, those that don't are so small they are of not nutritional value. In some species the male apparently hypnotises the female so that they can do the deed without risk. Now there's an idea.

Returning to the subject of food, spiders don't actually eat. Their prey has to be 'dissolved' because their gut cannot deal with solid food and indeed there are two filters between their mouth and stomach to ensure no solid food reaches it. Bizarre.

So, the next time you are out walking and there is dew on a spiders web, stop and take a good look at it, admire its beauty, and think about the effort that has been put into its construction. Don't destroy it, you may be signing the death warrant of a wonderfully creative lady spider who only lives as she does because that's way nature determined she should.

The 4 keys.

Hardly worth mentioning to be honest, spiders can get anywhere they want to, find shelter as and when they need it, if at all. Catch what they want, not much we can do to help there, and although they drink I don't think we can do much there either. Just celebrate them for being awesome.

Dragonfly

Dragonflies are magical, there is no doubt about that, a real wonder of the natural world. If you don't know it can only be because you haven't looked. Just venturing outside near water in summertime will reward you with great variety of rich colours, reds, blues, greens, browns and yellows and if you can get close enough to look at the wings, well, they have a beauty of natural design that is probably unparalleled.

The biggest dragonfly, the emperor, has a body that is approximately 8 cm long and a wingspan of about 10. Huge insects, any larger and I imagine they would not be able to fly. The body, a beautiful vivid blue on the male, paler on the female, is unmistakable as they hover skilfully quartering their territory looking for suitable insects to eat, from midges to prey as large as butterflies, they trap their dinner in between their ridged legs and consume it in flight.

The emperor is a hawker, the name given to the larger dragonflies due to their habitual behaviour of quartering the area over water, the smaller are known as darters, as they are seen rapidly moving from one place to another in straight lines, darting from here to there and then to there.

But eventually this stunningly beautiful dragonfly will land and this is just awesome. Dragonfly will land and spread his wings out at right angles to his body making it easy to study the beauty close up and amazingly, especially when you consider those large eyes give them 360-degree vision they will generally let you get pretty close too, and you need to, too, to study their beauty in any detail...

Take a moment and let your eyes feast on the delicate beauty of the patterns made by the veins (I'll call them veins) that give the wing it's strength. The basic design is the same for all species, they emanate from the base of the wing and are almost parallel along the forewing and curving back towards the rear of the wing, joined by a kind of cross vein, but like the fingerprints on our hands surely no two wings can be the same. Nature loves order, but just cannot repeat itself, naturally bespoke and exclusive. And the reason for this beauty is to stretch the lace like 'chitin' into place, extremely light, but strong enough to take the pounding of air caused by repeated wing beats that keep the insect airborne. Almost glassy, they set off the majestic body so well.

If we look further at the body there is a beauty of a completely different, dare I say, nature. The abdomen (tail bit) is made of repeated segments, again all similar, but just slightly different, patterns so intricate you can never quite make them out on the flying adult, you just get the colour and find yourself following the insect hoping that it will settle and allow you to move in for a close up, where with an emperor you will see blues emphasized by the black.

In fact, if you stop for a moment, and just reflect on the beauty of these insects and then think about the fact that we share this world with these creatures, that is a sobering thought in itself. They don't preen, they don't pose, they have no need of adornment of any kind, they just are, and are beautiful; that's it. That in itself is unreal too. And then look at the habitat they live in, that's pretty special as well. That's because of the life cycle they have that requires both water and air, or is it the environment that determined that life cycle.

Even more spectacular when you realise that these creatures were probably one of the first to step out of the water and become partly terrestrial.

Whichever way around it is, or was, it's pretty strange, wonderful and even inspirational. Nature is stranger and more beautiful than anything our imaginations can create. It is hard to imagine the alien lifecycle from the movie saga that 'alien' became, without the lifecycles we see in the insects on our own planet, ugly though they often are. There's a lovely line in one of the movies that Ripley states after the 'company' man tries to capture an alien for its monetary value back on earth at the expense of some of his crew mates, 'I don't know which species is worse, but you don't see them 'friggin' each other over for a percentage.' But once again I digress.

When your life cycle depends on you getting both in and out of the water and you're small, this presents certain difficulties which have to be overcome. Hard enough as a dragonfly, but even harder for a damselfly although the strategy operated by both is pretty much the same for leaving, it differs for returning the eggs though.

The main purpose for any adult of any organism, obviously, is to reproduce, from humans all the way down to the tiniest microbe. It's just that every species does it in a different way. Insects, and dragonflies, in this case, have a special adult stage that happens to be very different to its previous forms. Dragonflies, as large insects, get a fairly long time as an adult, a couple of months is possible and so also feed as adults; but spare a thought for the smaller ones, many of which don't even get mouthparts. The mayfly gets one day; think about it, one day. I imagine it's one hell of a one day, but still, it's one day.

Take a moment to think about quality of life over quantity of life; or maybe making the greatest quality of whatever life we have…

Incidentally, each adult only has to produce one offspring that survives to reproduce to maintain a healthy population, lots to think about there too, but another time.

So, having enjoyed a monumentally enjoyable time as an adult, for our dragonflies only the female has the responsibility of laying eggs in the water.

Damselflies take a different approach. After an energetic time in the air, they both take responsibility for getting the eggs into the water, and for some securely attached to something.

There is on the surface of water what appears to be a 'skin', called surface tension. If you look at water in a glass you see it as the water curves up the side of the glass where there is contact. No place here for the science, we don't have to worry about it, and nor do dogs, we are big. But for insects it is life determining. pond skater depends on it to 'skate' and if you look closely, you can see their feet kind of 'dent' the water. But dragonfly and damselfly have to penetrate it to get out as adults and also leave their eggs as they see fit. No mean feat.

So, as with any good marriage, they team up and do the job together. It's pretty much the last thing they will ever do and as it's their legacy they make an excellent job of it.

What is even more impressive, and as you'll have seen, it's a bit of a feature of the natural world, they do it innately, no one and nothing ever shows them how it's done, they just know. Can you imagine us as a species surviving with such a strategy, we wouldn't last a generation? Now there's a topic for a long discussion, but right now we're talking about dragonflies aren't we.

So, dragonflies have to penetrate this surface tension to lay their eggs, some do it by a good bit of ovipositing, such as most damselfly species.

The male grabs the female securely round the neck, yes, they do!!! Keeping his body straight. This will be for a number of reasons, first, obviously to assist the female in getting her eggs below the water, but also to stop any other male trying to have his wicked way with her. Jealousy then? Definitely. Not that that would stop him clearing off to find another female afterwards if he thinks he can manage it. Darters will also just lay the eggs under water, kind of dabbing them as they go.

Others such as the big female hawkers will climb back down the stem of a plant. She will then slice open a gap in a stem and deposit her eggs in it, actually laying the eggs in the stem of the plant.

Nature has some fabulous ways of overcoming difficulties in life.

Depending upon the time of year, the eggs will hatch after a few days, or wait for the following spring. Again, how does the nymph know, seasonal temperature change is far less significant in water than in air, there must be some trigger.

Anyway, the eggs hatch, out comes the small nymph, starving. After all, that is all the larval stage of any insect is, an eating machine, which is why many are laid on their food source. As dragonfly nymphs are carnivorous, they still have to catch theirs. The whole of the bottom jaw is telescopic, we're back to the analogy with alien again, and is hinged. When a suitable prey item swims passed it shoots out and draws its victim back to the nymph and it starts eating. Whatever it is, whether it's a small fish, tadpole or other insect larva. Dragonfly nymphs are one of the most aggressive predators in the water.

They like all insects have an exoskeleton, that is one that's on the outside, unlike us who have one on the inside, an endoskeleton. Ours thankfully grows with us, so we give it little more thought than that. In the case of our dragonfly nymph, it's a little different, as we shall see.

You see because it's on the outside, all the organs are loose and uncontained on the inside, but still growing. Eventually they need a new skeleton, exoskeletons once formed are hard and don't grow with the creature. What they do is grow another one on the inside and as it expands it hardens and the old one is shed and left behind. That is why when we go pond dipping with children, we find what appear to be dragonfly nymph 'skins'. They can shed their 'skin' up to 15 times whilst a nymph. It depends how long the nymph stage lasts for, which varies from species to species, from a few months, to up to 5 years for the Emperor we keep mentioning. The last change though has to be the most spectacular.

At dawn on a suitably sunny morning the nymph will leave behind it's last 'skin' and drag itself through the surface tension and leave the water. Whilst it waits for the sun to dry it, and it's wings out, it pumps them full of blood. And at just the right moment it takes to the air to begin the last part of its life cycle, as we mentioned earlier...

As I said, the most magnificent transformation.

So, the next question we must ask is, how do we bring them into our gardens? And that brings us back to the 4 keys once again.

The 4 keys

Access and Shelter

If there is a pond, lake or even a river in the locality then there is a fair chance they will find us, but active natural wonder seekers will want to be a bit more proactive than that and take some responsibility for bringing them into our gardens ourselves, and the answer is hopefully obvious. We need a pond, thus giving these magnificent insects all the niches, or special places they need for the entirety of their life cycle, and if it is brand new it will require a little while to establish, to have a good enough food supply for the nymph to feed.

A good sign is dying adults in late summer, this is a good indicator that they think your pond is suitable for their nymphs to find sufficient food and have thus laid their eggs in it. What an awesome sign of future life and reward for the hard work you have put into making and populating your pond.

A pond, like planting is an investment in the future.

Food and Water

Again, food for both the nymph and adult is mostly about the planting. As we have discussed above it's all in the food webs nature has constructed, put in the plants that the insects and other animals require, in the earth and the pond and eventually the food that a dragonfly needs will be abundant. Midges for example also grow in the pond and they are food for both adult and larval stages.

Water, well...

In summary

Whilst celebrating the life in our gardens is, on the surface of it, a most important 'thing' and gives us the biggest WOW moment going, we must look passed that and remember that we need these creatures in our lives at a basic survival level. As we mentioned earlier everything is dependent on everything else. If this was a scientific text this would be the place to get very theoretical and look at energy levels, take the whole food web thing into context and go to another level. Here it is enough just to know that all the plants and creatures can have a direct relationship with each other and it's about maintaining a healthy balance.

As stated in the trunk. Animals control animals, for example the relationship between a lynx and the hare. Without the lynx, number of hares grows very quickly. Thus, an arriving lynx will have lots of food to eat, and the numbers of lynx will expand. The number of hares will then decrease as the lynx catch and eat them. It then follows that the number of lynx will then reduce due to a shortage of food allowing the numbers of hare to once again expand and the cycle then repeats.

This relationship is the same between rabbits and the vegetation they eat and plants can also have a dramatic effect on the atmosphere on the planet which can influence the plants and animals, the lists and examples are endless.

With the ever-increasing loss of vegetation, for house building or agriculture for example, the need for our gardens to pick up as much of the shortfall as possible increases. And as has been discussed right through this book, the two most important things we can do as house and garden owners are install a pond and then look at the planting we put into our gardens and ponds. That is where the bit about food webs come in. What we can actually best do is provide a surplus of food in our gardens for the creatures we would like to see the most, or appreciate the most, because like it or not that will almost definitely plug so many gaps in the food web for so many creatures and that will increase and enrich our lives beyond measure.

It would be easy to just write a long list of plants here, but many plant species are mentioned above and essentially its simplest done at the design stage. Especially because then you can plan not only for the wildlife you want to bring in, but how you best can enjoy them whilst in your garden. Somewhere you can sit around a pond, especially if there is the sound of tumbling water is very relaxing as well as stimulating. Arranging the location of plants that display best from the places that you wish to sit makes best sense, and that may well be determined by how the sun moves through your garden and the time of day that you tend to use it.

As an added extra the planting you include at any stage of the evolution of your garden will change and evolve in itself as some plants always do better than you expect, some will die and as you visit gardens, garden centres and parks you will discover more plants that you like, and more importantly plants that insects, bees in particular, like. And of course, while you visit these places you will also see bird, animal and bug houses that will require you to buy them and install them too.

Ultimately, a garden is there to be enjoyed by you and a multitude of creatures, you are just the wise and beneficial curator overlooking your own benign dictatorship of creatures just doing their thing.

That is wonderful and very fulfilling.

Guardian

Somehow I'm looking for movement in shadows

More than random rustling in meadows

Looking to see if the past is still here

Believing in spirits without fear

Movement and rustling through trees

Something passing, more than just breeze

A sense of peace, a sense of place

There's nothing missing from the human race

If we look straight and true

Sense what is there, look and not stare

We matter not at all unless we sense our place

We are guardians, the human race

Part 3 Look for the learning.

Chapter 16.

What can we learn from the countryside?

Massive question. Learn from the countryside? Possibly not a question that many have ever really thought about. A bit like what have the Romans done for us really. It's not until you stop, and I mean actually stop, and use all your senses as described elsewhere in this book, and look, so to speak, that the examples are everywhere. And the more you look, the more you realise there is to learn. The examples are everywhere. In fact, the more considerations you make the more you will see. The answers are there to questions about pace, peace, context, connection, knowledge, differences, concepts and judgements to name a few. We are going to think about a few here. Whilst many of the examples are mentioned elsewhere in the book it is worthwhile collecting them altogether in one chapter, here...

First though, you will probably be aware there is a lot of use of the word depression these days, alongside mental health, more than ever before. Or at least so it seems to me. I imagine that's for many reasons, one of which is that it's more socially acceptable admitting you have a 'mental' condition or illness than ever before. That must be considered a good thing, obviously.

However, I feel it is also because we are the most disconnected generation ever. Probably because the very technology that was designed to bring us together has actually isolated us more than ever before. So many people are glued, almost addicted to their smart phones. You see it everywhere; people are walking along the road totally focussed on them, as a result their awareness has become reduced to that small space. Quite often they have headphones on and are listening to music or watching videos, isolating themselves further from the reality surrounding them. Have you ever sat in room full of people all engaged with their smart phones and not each other? We all have. I even know a couple who almost seem to text each other though Facebook whilst sitting next to each other on the same sofa.

It is likely that two of the myriad of reasons causing depression are lack of 'meaningful human relationships' and disconnection from nature.

I know many people who have no interest in being outside at all, want nothing from the countryside, nature or their garden, or come to that, even want a garden. It then follows that, some are and will be happy or 'numb', in their isolation, desired or not. But many are not and will only admit it to themselves, if at all. There's a lot of people living a kind of half-life without actually realising it.

To a certain extent, even our energy efficient homes isolate us from the energy giving weather, we can't even hear and sometimes not even see the wind and rain. It's important to make the choice to shelter, rather than not being aware of our outdoor environment.

When discussing how we might address this issue I have often been heard to utter the phrase, 'those who need us the most, want us the least'. And it is a hard one to crack, if you have any ideas, please get in touch.

So, if we could persuade those who are addicted to their insular technology to come outside, what would they have the chance to realise if they would take that first step?

The first thing would be to just take in deep breath of fresh air, usually cool in England. Their bodies do it automatically anyway. Our bodies still remember, even if our minds have forgotten. That alone is the first step to feeling better and more alive. And acknowledging that fact is in itself a huge release.

Second just go for a walk. A mile is enough. At first. Actions cures things (ACT), as my business coach can often be heard to state. Movement will always help, whatever the situation. After a while stop and take in the scenery around you. Just enjoy everything that is there. The view, the vegetation, any birds you see, or hear. Maybe some insects, or maybe even an animal. Don't worry about what it is called, or at least what we've called it. It really doesn't matter. Just enjoy the sense of space, take in everything you can see and actually acknowledge that this is a world that you are a part of, whether you want to accept it or not. You are!

Names are not important. Whilst it's great to know what things are called, especially for a discussion; although not knowing does add an extra element to a chat, it really does not matter. I mean, think about it. An oak tree doesn't know it's an oak tree, it doesn't even care. You might say 'yes, but that's because an oak tree can't think.' I would answer, 'how do you know that?', but that's another discussion. Take for example a fox, a fox can think and it doesn't know that it's a fox, and likewise, cares even less. It also doesn't care that the dinner it's trying to catch is called a rabbit. Any more than the rabbit knows or cares that it is called a rabbit, or that a fox is trying to catch it, or that it might become, or be called, dinner. Names are a human preoccupation. It is, it would seem, part of our need to feel we are at the top of any system, classification, food chain of other man-made invention or convention to give everything a name and put it in its place, according to us. That is in many ways healthy as long as we keep ourselves in context.

The fox is more concerned with being what it is and what it does, foxness rather than being a fox. A rabbit is just concerned with getting on with life as it is around it.

Think about the world as it is now. Not yesterday or tomorrow. Have you ever noticed anything, creature, plant or tree show any real observation of anything apart from now? The simplest example is your own dog. When it sees a dog coming there is usually excitement to run off and play, which depending upon the level of training it has, and your tolerance of dog behaviour, it may be allowed to do, but as soon as that other dog is behind it, it's history and forgotten. Obviously, there are exceptions, but for most of the plants and animals out there, there is just a sense of now.

And that is the next big thing we can learn from our wonderful outdoors, just appreciate the wonderful world we live in. That is a twofold observation. Firstly, simply, that we are a part of this wonderful and magical world. That is cause for celebration itself. I mean, for all our abilities to look and search space, and realise just how mind blowing big it is and I mean absolutely much bigger than you can possibly imagine. As far as we can tell, this is the only planet with life on it, or at least life as we can accept it is at this moment in our development. The odds have to suggest there must be some more life somewhere in this universe, but so far, we haven't found it and it hasn't found us. That maybe for the best...

One of the main causes or factors in being depressed maybe due to putting too much emphasis on oneself. And whilst it pays to be aware of how wonderful we are, realising just how insignificant we are in the great and wonderful world we are a part of surely puts that thought into perspective. The world does not orbit around us, we are not the centre of it. We are just a very small part of it, in the greater scheme of things.

The outdoors, nature, Mother Earth, or whatever name or consideration we want to give it, her, him, is a real EGO killer, or EGO putter in its place thing. Celebrate rather than frustrate. It will be here long after we have gone, and probably as a result of our own meddling. Whilst I don't know for sure, it seems very likely that COVID began in one form or another in a man-made laboratory. Who came up with the atomic bomb, or whatever the latest terror is?

The scheme of things then leads us to the next realisation. Everything operates according to its niche in the grander scheme of things. Food chains and webs are discussed more fully in chapter 15, but there are other factors too. Every organism functions and operates in a fairly narrow window of conditions that it has adapted to survive in and they will determine what it does and where. What temperature range suits it best? Whether it breathes through air or water, or both? Lives in one, or the other, or both? What it eats and how it gains water to quench its thirst? What time of day it is most active?

Again, most living things have no conscious awareness of these needs, but just functions superbly well amongst them. They don't even worry about our activities to change the course of natural events.

Hopefully by now you will have realised that to see, hear, smell, touch and taste this world enough to have some appreciation you have used your senses in varying degrees to make these observations. It then follows that something allows you to use these senses and make thoughts based on them. That obviously, is your brain, your mind. It takes all the information we feed into it and processes it, both consciously and unconsciously. Usually whether we want it to or not. Mostly that is for the good. Imagine if you had to remember to breathe or make your heart beat. So much of what we do is on autopilot. We also make important decisions based on our immediate environment, whether we are too hot, too cold, hungry, thirsty, need sleep or whatever.

All sentient creatures do this, all the time. The difference is that we add an extra element to this thought. We add in a lot of our past that we carry around with us, along with our judgements based on that past and then make prejudgments based on our interpretation of that past. What we believe the future will be. Which if you then look back, you'll realise are often wrong. We spend a lot of time thinking, 'I'll be happy when…' which never seems to be quite as we want, or we want something more. All the life that is in the world around us just focusses on 'now'. There is no prejudgment in nature. Anywhere. A tide rolls up the beach, the wind blows, the fox chases the rabbit because that is what is, that is it. It's evolved to operate perfectly in the niche it lives in, but put it in a different place and it would struggle, a bit like the American Indians we discussed in chapter 2.

Whilst we need to have things to look forward to, learning to enjoy the wait, living in the now, is just as important. Make plans, have goals, but enjoy the wait.

Now, there is an important distinction to be made here. Whilst giving a presentation on this very subject recently I was challenged on this subject. An attendee raised his hand to ask a question. 'You're telling me a fox doesn't prejudge the wind and the movement of scent, the distance of the rabbit, the speed of the rabbit, compared to itself.' I have to admit, at first, it was a great question, but when you think about it, no the fox doesn't. It makes judgements based on all those factors and then decides whether or not to give chase. It may even then react to the way the hunt is going and make another judgement.

But it doesn't ever make a decision based on whether the world, or a specific person will like it, or do something. It doesn't overthink the end result, what will happen if I do this, or even think, 'this didn't work last time, so I am not going to do it again.' No decisions get made with half the information or dodgy interpretation of the all the information to hand. That is a human condition. There is no hiding from any perceived consequence of any action. There is a massive difference between judgement and pre judgement.

There is only one creature on this planet that ever thinks about ending life, and that is us. This was most evident on a recent visit to a local woodland. A large silver birch had fallen over, probably during a storm or hurricane. It still had some roots in the ground and just carried fighting for life as it had always done. Every branch now became a new trunk, thickening and searching for the sun so as to continue life as it had always done.

Wouldn't it be wonderful if we could learn to enjoy and celebrate life in the here and now, without prejudgment, as every other organism in our world does?

Watch birds at a bird feeder. Some will take seed directly from the feeder, usually those that are good at balancing on a small perch. Sparrows, blue and great tits for example. They tend to be very messy, and a lot of food generally falls onto the floor. There, the birds that find it hard to negotiate the feeder will feed. Dunnocks, blackbirds and robins for example. They eat the food they find where they can best access it. Not one bird refuses any food because another bird has had it in its mouth or touched it or makes any judgement about the food based on where it's come from. Some creatures, such as dung beetles, have adapted to clear up the rotting leftovers and thank heavens for them, our world would be a very unpleasant place if they weren't here. Again, no prejudgment. It's just food.

Now the point I was looking to make here before I allowed myself to be distracted was that there is something 'in' us that we can't define. That spark we discussed in chapter 2.

And if we then return to that heartbeat, there's another lesson to learn. Everything on this planet has a heartbeat of some kind. Everything. Some of them may operate so slowly we are not aware of it, but if we stop for a moment and let the world around us enter our conscious, we can just about begin to perceive it.

Plants, trees in particular, have a great need to pump sap around their bodies, just as we have a need to pump blood around ours. The fact is trees are so good at it they can pump sap sometimes one to two hundred meters up into the twigs and leaves at their very top. Think of the height of a redwood tree. Even today with our technical abilities we still cannot raise water to those heights with an efficiency that comes close to the ability of a tree. Humbling once again. Empathy with our world should inspire humility.

On the subject of trees, there's another vital lesson, that we can all learn. Flexibility. Whilst if there is enough pressure, we all fall down, if we are flexible, it's easier to absorb the everyday pressures of life. The heating not working, people who break promises, losing a job for example are life pressures that can upset us or make life difficult, but if, like trees, we can let things pass, bend like a tree, let them blow through like the wind through a tree then life becomes simpler. The quicker we can let the storm go the more fully we can enjoy our short lives. Or be like the birch mentioned just now, it had a life altering event but carried on doing the best it could to live life as fully as possible.

And that reminds us that all life is determined by cycles. We have already discussed the physical cycles of day and night, lunar, seasonal and annual cycles, but we also have emotional cycles that are determined by our reaction to that events that unfurl around us. Like the cycles mentioned, there is a time for joy, there is a time for sadness, there is a time for high adventure and a time for tranquillity, just as there is a time for day and a time for night etc. Whilst we should try and keep them all in perspective so that we can live full and rewarding lives, we need to experience the lows and the highs to enjoy the emotions we would like to spend the majority of our time in. You've got to go there to come back or lose something to find it again.

As Thomas Wayne said to his son, after he fell down the well, 'Why do we fall down Bruce? So we can learn to pick ourselves back up'.

On the subject of weathering the storm, if you look around you, you will notice that there is nothing in a hurry. The only time anything gets in a hurry in our world is when it is trying to catch dinner or evade becoming dinner. Otherwise, every organism just moves at its most efficient pace, whether that's growing, moving from A to B, catching the next meal, or building a home. Nothing wastes energy unnecessarily. Have you ever watched Buzzard spiralling on then thermals? They use air that is rising to carry them to great height and then fly off to wherever from that height. Thus saving energy and unconsciously working at their most efficient. There's a natural pace to life. You will have noticed when out walking, our own natural paces are all different. Some of us have to adjust, but ultimately it's much easier to just go with the natural cycles when we can. Imagine if you are a channel swimmer, it is a lot easier to reach your destination if the tide is with you, rather than against. Use this philosophy at work, in a hobby, but possibly most importantly when making any decision. Nothing is quite as overwhelmingly important if you have taken a little time to think it through if you can. Let the thought process move at a natural pace.

It doesn't matter what you want, you have to just let it happen. That's a tricky one to get your head around. Look at this way, you may want to go to sleep, you can't make it happen, you have to let it happen at its own pace. The same is true for a garden, you can design it. You can construct the hard landscaping, you can put the plants in, but then you have to let it the plants grow. Gardens don't mature overnight.

Remember, you must trust in the process. You are not in control. You never were and never will be. You can make decisions on your immediate environment, but ultimately your end is already pre-determined, it's just how you go with the natural pace of life that will determine the value of the life you have.

Put simply, enjoy now, at the pace that is natural. Never get too focused on the bad stuff, or what you have not got, the good is always coming. Have gratitude and appreciation for the amazing world we live in. Accept it for what it is but ask questions. Enjoy change. Have patience, never prejudge and trust. Your responsibility is to be happy as much of the time as you can just as long as its not at the expense of others. Unless of course in the greater scheme of things they are your dinner.

Chapter 17.

So, what do I do?

I don't have an altar, or a strict code of conduct or any special artefacts, but I do have a morning routine which might be called a ritual and I guess it is of sorts, but it is evolving and personal. It works for me. I have talked to others about it, but not with any intention of them following it, but to work out what works for them.

So, what's my morning routine, which I follow most days of the week, not every day, and not really in company, but most days? It sets up my day and has increasingly begun to pervade the way I operate and function through the day, it even helps me to sleep well at night and there is a lot to be said for that. In fact, a good night's sleep might be the single greatest factor of all that I have written here. And certainly better than any drug, natural or contrived that we have ever taken, willingly or not.

It's all about balance for me, and as you might have noticed, finding that balance out of doors as often as possible. It all just makes more sense out there, to me at least.

So firstly, spiritual balance which fits nicely into the morning walk I do with the dogs. I've always enjoyed the dawn, and often the last hour or two of darkness in winter. I hate getting up early, but the rewards are often spectacular. Dawn is the most beautiful time of day, to see the light begin to find its way back into our world once more and light up the clouds as it does so is sublime, a simple form of connection. There's a little magic in the world and if we allow ourselves, we can feel it. Often the creatures we share our world with are also just getting up too, birds most audibly. You can see silhouettes in the sky, or catch something moving as they alight, usually just after you've walked passed them. That's where the phrase bird brain might have come from, the danger has passed by then. Or the rustling of a mouse in a hedgerow. In the spring the birdsong is beautiful. The world seems to be alive and in love... But also, there are those creatures who have finished their activities and are going home or roosting up, owls or hedgehogs to name two. Or the joy of watching scruffy our terrier chasing Canada geese hopelessly as they circle overhead. It is, as I said a magical time.

It is the time I choose to say, well, usually shout out my gratitude's to whoever or whatever may be listening.

I begin by saying hello and good morning to spirit, the tao, the world and the people of the Fae, the four directions, the upper worlds, gods, angels and archangels, Gabriel, Uriel, Michael and Raphael and the lower worlds where our ancestors reside, animal and spirit guides before finishing off once more with the spirit, or Tao that glues this whole world and spiritual experience together and I then acknowledge everything I am grateful for, this world, everything on it, plant, animal, bugs and fungi, the air we breathe in the first instance. Then my house and my garden, my bed and food to eat. Those that make my house a home, my wife and my sons; all my family, especially the grandkids. My business, the leads I get and those that become my clients, even the difficult ones. My coach and those I network with that support me. My creativity, my ability to live a full life of giving, the money I have in the bank. Enough obviously, without getting greedy. My love of this life. A sample prayer follows this chapter.

214

On my return, I turn my attention to the physical, flexibility and balance. I have a routine I go through, well three actually. The first I have developed that requires a little skill and flexibility that has developed from the original exercises I started with. The second intersperses elements of the Chinese discipline of Quigong and basic circuit training exercises all designed to exercise all parts of the body. The latter two I use on alternating days, the former I do every day.

My main routine has become firmly based in the cycles which fits the thinking that everything is part of a cycle, and the fact that it evolved rather than being designed fits nicely too.

I begin with my hands together in front of me, head bowed, a salutation to spirit, that thing that is life, before moving to a standard Yoga tree pose, one leg raised to the knee on the other and my hands raised above my head and together. I lower my hands to a standard pose of prayer. I hold this pose for a count of eleven.

Whilst still balancing on the same leg I then contract my whole body, other leg and arms into as tightly compacted ball as I can. I also hold again, for a count of eleven. This pose I call the egg, physical form begins.

I then move my arms out like wings reaching out as far as possible, hands and fingers outstretched and my elevated leg behind me as a tail, foot pointing behind me and I look forwards. This I call the bird, in the flight of life.

The final pose, if I am on my right leg, I rotate right with my upper body, leg out straight in line and arms perpendicular, adopting a star pose. A star representing life after the end of physical form before life begins again. Again, I hold for a count of eleven with both of these poses.

I then repeat the entire cycle again on the other foot. And repeat this process for eleven repetitions as well. Each day I change the foot I begin with so ultimately each foot is treated equally. It can be difficult to count accurately whilst exercising, so I also rotate through the four corners of the world as I go, thus I can always work out where I am. I also change progression of the routine sometimes working backwards on one leg, thus the routine for each leg becomes a mirror of the other, further introducing balance.

For me it is a set of positions that as I move through them represent the cycle of life, another level of connection that evolved very naturally for me.

Whilst focusing on the body, we should always listen for the signs and signals it gives us. We need our pains, they let us know of the things, or conditions that we should address. Avoid taking pain killers for a headache for example. Treat the source, not the symptom. A headache is often a sign that we are dehydrated, or that there is pressure somewhere else that we are not aware of. The better we treat our body the better the signals it will give us.

Next, I read from two books, currently one called "Everyday Nature' by Andy Beer. It has an entry for every day, based on a potential observation relative to the time of year. And then I focus on whichever essay is relevant to that week from the Tao Te Ching, currently as interpreted by Wayne Dyer in his book 'Change your thoughts, change your life.' I focus on an essay for a week at a time. Often underlining anything that strikes a chord that day, and it is always something different each day.

I then venture out into the garden to meditate on whatever struck me as important during my reading. I sit by the pond as a rule, but venture into the shelter of the pergola if it is raining. Being outside, meditating or not is powerful in rain, but only if you are not getting wet. I also try to be mindful of the world around me whilst meditating, especially with magpies nesting above me at the moment (spring 2021). We are always more receptive to any stimulus when outdoors. It boosts our connectivity to our world too.

Have you ever tried moving forward and backwards with your upper body as you meditate? There's a natural rhythm within us and if we match this rocking with our resting breath the experience can become even more powerful. Don't necessarily keep your eyes shut either, opening them from time to time potentially gives you an insight into another reality, maybe...

For me, this routine is a vital component of my spiritual routine, providing spiritual, physical and mental balance. My internal white noise is greatly reduced with the growth of internal peace and tranquility. Like anything, consistency is important if you wish to grow with any skill or habit, as well growing in fluency and expertise. Whilst regular routine is vital, so is a rest, enjoy not doing any routine that works for you as much as you do it.

It's all one long meditation really!

Enjoy being set up for the day.

Why always a count of eleven? Eleven is the universal number. It's a power number, carrying spiritual enlightenment. A prime number that cannot be divided. That when it becomes evident usually carries news of great portent. Is often used to signify haste or importance. The eleventh hour. Or as in World War One, peace came on the eleventh hour of the eleventh day of the eleventh month.

It is also a number that just feels right. More right than ten anyway.

If I need to be quiet and journey shamanically, (meditation on a question) or just meditate. I will sit in my office on my round carpet with candles lit for the four directions and light one in front of me, I may invoke sacred space, I may set up a drumming tape to accompany me, and I'll sit for as long as I have, or need to sit.

If I have time, I will go to one of my sitting spots and sit quietly there, again for as long as I have or need to. I also join in with one or two online meditation groups.

I try to keep my thoughts on a high vibration, always looking for the positive. Anything unhelpful or negative I readjust as quickly as possible. For example, a few weeks ago at a show I present only three people turned up for an event. Obviously at first, I was disappointed and a little embarrassed, for our guest as well as myself. But quickly I realised that I wasn't going to let the absence of other people determine my state of happiness and thus focussed on our guest and those that were there.

It thus follows that keeping anxiety at bay is also a choice (for most of us) and is most easily addressed by taking responsibility for our own actions, but I said that in the first book didn't I!

It's also quite possible that the best way to find inner peace within is by looking without and learning from the world around us. The lessons we need are all there. This may be why we think most effectively and feel most alive when we are outside.

Looking back, I think I was looking to find that inner peace and calm all along, and a lot of what I have written about I was doing or had already started looking for anyway. I just didn't know it. Love for the land was almost always there. I've never been that great a socialite, but I love to feel I belong to a small, trusted group of people. Gratitude is talked about by many of those around me, chosen because they lift me up. The exercises came to me during a shamanic journey and has grown since those early messages. The Tao was recommended during discussion with my business coach, and Everyday Nature was a gift. Both put in my path for a reason. The beginnings of meditation, for me, is explained in 'the Three Year Pond', but the need and practice has increased with understanding.

The 41st verse of the Tao te Ching talks about great, middling and inferior scholars with regard to understanding the Tao and the way. I'd like to think I am somewhere between middling and great, getting there, but having a long way still to go...

There can be no emotion without a thought to precede it. And who is control of our thoughts? We are. And ultimately what are thoughts?

Well, energy, obviously.

Happiness is a choice. Always.

A prayer for the morning.

Good morning World.

Good morning Spirit.

Good morning to the Tao.

Good morning to The All.

Good morning to the People of the Fae.

Good morning to all elementals.

Good morning to Earth in the North. *(Give a salutation to the North)*.

From where springs all life, taking energy from the Sun and making food to eat and air to breathe.

Giving a home to the connecting fibres of Fungi, as well as worms and ants and other earth dwellers.

All the plants, trees, hedgerows, flowers and food crops.

And also to all the herbivores that eat the plants that grow.

Good morning to Air in the East. *(Give a salutation to the East).*

Giving that life breath, giving that life a voice and a medium for that voice to be made and heard.

To all the creatures that live in air, birds, bats and insects as well as the bugs and virus'.

Good morning to Fire in the South. *(Give a salutation to the South),* giving that life passion for life and to celebrate living.

To have imagination, creativity and the power to bring balance to the world.

And to the creatures that help us to bring balance. The carnivores.

Good morning to Water in the West. *(Give a salutation to the West),*

Quenching the thirst of that life, washing that life, washing the Earth.

Providing habitat to all the creatures that live in water, from the highest clouds to the deepest oceans and everything in between, seas, lochs, lakes, rivers, pools and streams

And the massive variety of life that lives in water.

To the upper worlds, to the gods, teachers, angels and archangels.

To Gabriel in the North. Angel of good news.

Thank you for all good news and giving me the power to keep the news good.

Uriel in the East. Angel of light, and keeper of the doors to the kingdom.

May divine light shine on me and keep information and inspiration flowing.

Michael in the South, Angel of protection.

I thank you for divine protection and for the angels assigned to look out for me.

Raphael in the West, Angel of love and healing.

I thank you for divine love and divine healing.

Good morning to all in the lower worlds.

My ancestors.... *(insert yours here).*

My animal guides.... *(insert yours here).*

Any power animals, spirit guides or ethereal beings I don't know of...

I thank you.

And in the centre, *(said circling, giving a salutation to the whole world)*, Great Spirit, the Tao, the All for making and holding everything in this world together.

I thank you.

And then give gratitude for anything you are grateful for, your home, your life, your wife, your family, leads, clients, your job..... It's up to you. And make a request for anything you'd like to receive, put it out there...

Chapter 18.

In Conclusion

So what does all this mean?

Firstly, if everything is based on cycles then maybe we should look back to the American Indians and live in circles. Look around you now. Right now. What do you have around you that is circular? We live in rectangular rooms, that fit into rectangular houses, that are arranged on rectangular roads. We sleep in rectangular beds. We drive rectangular cars. The list is endless and whilst it is a slightly generic statement, you get the picture. The Americans, who took the land away from the Indigenous Indians are possibly the worst, with their towns and cities arranged in blocks...

Everything else in our world still adheres to the cycles that occur naturally. From the smallest 'thing' that we can find, 'quarks' that make up protons and neutrons, in quantum mechanics that make up the components of atoms to the largest universes that we know of. The only thing that changes is scale. That word has occurred once or twice here too.

And as I understand it everything that exists or has ever existed vibrates....

The natural world has everything in it we need, all we have to do is look and remember. Two major causes of depression are disconnection from the world around us and a lack of meaningful human connection. All other creatures are very connected and have meaningful connection with others of their species as they have evolved to do. Even those that live in social groups, it has been shown, never lower themselves into depression the way humans do. It has also been shown that those living in the countryside never get as depressed as those living in towns and cities. Interesting.

We are possibly the first generation, or two, that has isolated ourselves almost completely from the world we live in. Our smart phones, the most amazing means of connecting us together have possibly isolated ourselves in ways never seen before.

If we connect with our countryside, we realise our ego is misinformed, the world does not orbit around us, we are a small part of a much bigger world. The countryside expands horizons. It becomes obvious that we are part of everything, we are connected. Everything has a heartbeat, all animals, birds, insects, plants and trees. Trees are the most amazing pumps of liquid on the planet and what is a heart in its simplest form, but a pump?

Everything else in our world lives at a pace that is determined by natural law, it moves in the most efficient way, doesn't waste energy unless there is a likely reward such as a meal or a place to live. All creatures know that they must roll with the changes, hide up when it rains other than to catch food, and even that is weighed and measured, and be most productive when the weather is appropriate. Those that do not apply what they have learnt do not survive. If you can't catch food, you will starve.

It then follows though that you need to be flexible. Have you ever wondered how trees stay upright through a hurricane or other extreme form of weather when they have such a small root stock compared to their height? A one-hundred-meter-high tree will often have root ball of just a few meters in diameter. They bend, it's as simple as that.

Some trees, palm trees for example, can bend almost to the ground and then return to their usual position. A lot to be learnt there too. If we can be flexible, especially in our relations with those around us life would be so much more enjoyable.

And that brings us to one of the most important lessons our countryside can teach us. Stop making pre judgements. We are the only species making decisions, usually regarding other people with only fragments of information to go on. Smart phones, which should help eliminate this are possibly the worst feeder of judgements made poorly. We should now be able to keep each other informed better now than ever before. The examples are numerous, but simply, think about it. When was the last time you made a decision because someone hadn't called or phoned you when they should have done and you made a prejudgement based on that information? Usually, the one that you want the least because we all have overactive imaginations.

Probably not that long ago. And then discovered that they had let their battery go flat. Easily done. Or their judgement of a situation was different to yours. Your date didn't turn up because something had happened and they left their phone at home or had dropped it. Or you had been so busy trying to phone them that they couldn't get through to you. The list is endless.

I doubt I will ever have the conviction to follow one way or one path, or one religion. As I have outlined above, I have been immersing myself in all kinds of spirituality for a long time now and I am probably part way along a path that works for me right now, but will I am sure continue to evolve as long as I am here to evolve it. Not sure how I would describe myself, but I am not a Christian, Hindu, Muslim, Buddhist or any other religion or philosophy. I kind of feel comfortable with Pagan, especially if the definition is countryman... but I'm not 100% with that either.

Why is Pagan, or druid maybe, so close? A pagan takes responsibility for all his actions and for the environment around him. It's about harbouring a desire to learn from and understand as much as possible from the world around us. It is about living in harmony as far as is possible with the natural cycles of life, the tides, the seasons and every other inhabitant of our wonderful world. Receiving, as well as possible, the messages all around, whether literal or metaphorical in all ways and accepting all gifts as an opportunity to learn. I think I do that! I certainly try to.

Or alternatively, and just as likely, I resonate with all of them. There is something I love about all the philosophies I have studied.

I am a dabbler!

What is clear to me though is as follows. I definitely believe there is something greater than all of 'us' out there, whether it is conscious or not; whether it is an integral part of everything, one soul or like a large umbrella that we are all linked to I don't know for sure, but I have my suspicions. I firmly believe that there is something that is pervading, that exists for all time, there is no way that our 'souls' just spring into life and then disappear when we die. I don't know whether we have an eternal purpose or not, but that there is both divine will and free will makes sense. That likelihood that when both are the same allows more to be accomplished feels right and experience, for me, proves this. The probability that we receive messages, through dreams, meditations or shamanic journeys, or even the countryside around us should we choose to look also makes sense and experience also confirms this.

Here's an example.

It was during the autumn of 2019. It began on the Monday, we knew we were going to be away for a couple of days to Little Mistletoe, the place I mentioned above, the following weekend.

On the Monday, whilst having a cuppa with my wife we both felt some significant change was coming. We had no idea what or why, but we both felt it, and knew it. Indeed, it was my wife who stated it.

The next day, Tuesday, I was one of my regular morning walks. I saw a buzzard, it was close, really close, within 10 meters close, it had been sitting in the elder bushes by the path and Scruffy the dog had spooked it. One on one day would have been awesome, but for the act to be repeated a day later, Wednesday, really got my attention.

Call it what you like, the appearance of buzzards pretty much always prescribes something good is about to happen or point me to a decision I need to make. So, at this point my attention is roused. In the same way, a prolonged period without a buzzard in my life will cause me to look around and see what I am missing, because the signs are always there.

Thursday wasn't a buzzard though. Whilst out on the pergola meditating, a bell, a small bell was ringing. We have wind chimes out there, but no bells, and yes it could have been next door, but I had never heard it before, and I've not heard it since. Something was definitely looking to gain my attention.

On Friday though what I saw was spectacular. It was a beautiful autumn day, little wind and the heat of the sun warming in an unobtrusive manner. The sun bright enough without burning into your eyes as it does in summer. I was walking towards Sholden across the Downs, along a footpath, that cut the stubble strewn field in half when suddenly there arose a spectacular parliament of rooks, several hundred strong. From behind I could see another bird, that at first, I thought was another rook, flying straight towards me. As this bird kept coming it became very clear that this wasn't another rook. Whilst still appearing to be black, and having fingers on the ends of it wings, as does a rook, its real size was starting to become clear as the perspective of distance was reduced. It was almost hanging in the air and appeared almost as a Klingon Bird of Prey from Star Trek, over the horizon, as it continued it's path towards me, relentlessly moving forward. The bird, a buzzard, a big female, brown and imposing, made her way slowly enough that I could take photographs and even shoot a video to help me get my messages across to the big wide world.

In fact, I only lost track of her when, my neck having bent as far back as it could, I had to turn around and I had to look away from my camera to find her again as she flew over the trees in the churchyard and then vanished over the church.

Now it is enough just to enjoy that spectacle at face value, because buzzards are awesome, big and spectacular and to be that close is special in its own right.

But for me, there was more. Call it a message, call it gut feeling, call it sixth sense, call it what you will, there was more. I knew it then and looking back on it in hindsight I should have had more faith. Again, let me explain.

Without going into reems of great detail, there were things I knew had to change, things I was doing, things what I wanted to do, should or had to do. Coincidence was huge, my wife and I were, as I said, going away for a planning weekend, that day.

We even made big plans for change, and then at the last minute backed away from that decision because it was a big one and quite frankly, we got scared. Big changes often require faith and a lot of belief (freewill and divine will?). Looking back, had we made the changes we would have saved quite a lot of money, thousands in fact, never mind the time as well, because ultimately events unfolded that meant our decision would have been the right one and eventually happened anyway. We didn't have the faith to follow divine will even though we knew it made sense. Now we are clearly on that path that we should have set in motion that weekend. Remember freewill, any guidance given has to treated responsibly. You never have to follow advice blindly. All actions should be still made skillfully.

And what was the actual message that I received that day, set the path that you know is right and do not lose sight of the end goal.

So, sixth sense, gut feeling, message or just massive self-mind job? It doesn't matter, have gratitude and faith and the decision is easy.

I think if we just thought of ourselves as all a part of the same 'species' who all eat similar foods, drink similar drinks, bleed in the same way, have bodies that are all made or constructed the same way and took a little time to recognise every difference ultimately is superficial, and as I remember David Bowie stating, 'differences should be celebrated rather than victimised', then life for everybody could be much more pleasant. That is treat ourselves, those around us and even those we don't know with a little more love and respect.

The Buddhist practice of metta bhavana gives a great practice for this. Metta means universal love, friendliness and kindness or loving kindness. Bhavana is development or cultivation. It is a five-stage process, a meditation for each.

First, for yourself. Focus on your inner peace, your strength and your ability to love, both yourself and the world around you. Next, for a good friend. Wish for the good health and the ability to make choices based on love of themselves, their friends and again the world around them, think about what gives that connection to be good friends. Third, someone you do not particularly like or have difficulty dealing with in a positive manner, wish for them good things and possibly look to address your feelings toward them, often the feeling is just a result of misinterpretation of actions or words. And possibly not intended.

Fourth, an enemy or someone of mindset and opinion you don't or can't understand. Do not get involved with hatred or anger, that will just weigh you down. Offer them love and goodwill and hope they will find love too. How can you use anger with compassion?

Forgiveness is in two parts. First, for yourself so that you don't carry anger around with you, you don't even have to tell them. And second, for them, say, 'I forgive you'. Which is for them. You might never be good friends, you may never forget. They may not want the gift, but give it to them anyway.

And fifth, everyone in the world. All those above and everyone of any religion, faith, creed, belief, colour or whatever. Offer the whole world love.

Thus bring the meditation to a close. The hardest one is the first, because without peace love and kindness for yourself, how can you achieve anymore?

Wouldn't the world be a great place if we could all agree to be 'nice' to each other.

So, faith and gratitude I believe are the bedrock of civilisation, the bedrock of inner peace, calm and responsibility.

Anyway, back to the point or the question I posed above before I got distracted. Whilst I don't know and who can? I suspect the answer, ultimately, is there and straight forward really. Simple, even. Remember the analogy between our brains and the way they work with signals (or energy) making their way up and down our nerve pathways to and from the relevant receptors all over our bodies and the comparison of how our brains work to the way our countryside works, passing energy from the sun and to all creatures, and how all the creatures interact with each other and all the plants and animals also interact on this planet, and then how they all are dependant and interact with the gases that also permeate our bodies and the atmosphere. Everything is connected, interconnected, dependent upon and part of one great whole.

Imagine if we all thought that we are a part of a greater whole, albeit with a feeling of 'self' whilst we also had a physical body and that the only thing that was actually different was that physical body. I think everybody would treat everyone a little better, don't you?

And then there's the analogy to the Earth itself. I repeat the description I used before.

The soil is the skin, rocks the skeleton, the atmosphere the lungs, bodily fluids formed of seas and rivers, oil as blood, nature (all life) makes up the brain and the earths molten core the heart.

It makes sense and it feels right too. Gut feeling? The sixth sense?

So, physically definitely, but I think also spiritually. After all our bodies don't work without something to drive them, and I think ultimately there must be connection there too. Nothing can exist happily in isolation. The population, any population cannot exist if we are all isolated, it will die out. All life needs life, needs connection. More than that need to feel a part of something. Something bigger and have a purpose. Why else do we have freewill if not to grow. Why else do we feel so satisfied for reasons we cannot fathom. Why do we feel good when we help and treat others and ourselves with love and respect?

I believe we are all connected, everything is connected in every way we can imagine. Physically, spiritually, philosophically, biologically, dare I say religiously. Our world will endure with us and without us, or any other creatures as it has done for millennia and will continue for millennia to come. Any positive effort to connect and balance ourselves and completely interact with our world will result in a well-balanced and connected and ultimately fulfilled 'soul'. Do we come back? Difficult to say.

Many of the issues we must deal with, such as depression, as we have discussed are based on a possibly over active ego, or a feeling of disconnection. Just engaging in an activity such as going for a walk will help massively. Putting ourselves in an outside space, in nature immediately gives us a sense of connection, it reduces our sense of self-importance because we can easily realise we are not the centre of the world, but a part of it. Landscape builds us up. We cannot change it, we are not in control of it, but the lessons are there if we just look.

As a friend of mine, a Buddhist, told me, our bodies completely renew themselves every seven years, so we are in a state of flux all the time. If we imagine our souls as candle flames, each flame can never be repeated, so therefore neither can a soul. And that kind of fits the umbrella principle of a soul too. All the bits go back, but then get mixed up in a kind of spiritual soup before returning…

We just need to be, feel and acknowledge the connection that we have, or had and need to rekindle once more. Maybe if we stopped mucking about with the genetics of 'things', it might help. We were designed to eat foods the way they are grown and have evolved. Our plants evolved to be in such as a form as works. The pretty flowers we have mutated for stronger colours are infertile, surely there is a message there too.

It would be great if we could all agree to help our world be the safe place we need and are entitled to, and have, if we could leave it alone. Let it heal itself. The evidence is there to see if we look. Especially after the 2020 lockdown.

The same principle physically and spiritually continues wherever we 'look'.

Whilst we need to be connected to this world, it thus follows that we need to be ready to change, after all evolution is likely a driving factor in our unconscious existence and that needs to be mental as well as spiritual and that means we have to be tolerant of all things and all people and all beliefs at all times. Our history is full of what happens when we are intolerant, the crusades, witch hunts of medieval times, or conquests of those considered less 'civilised. White man versus the American Indian, or the English colonising the Indians, the Chinese over running Tibet, or the slavery of African tribes. The list is endless.

I guess we should remember that our physical bodies are just guests on this world, just as we are guest in our friends' houses, or our work places or a cottage when we are on holiday. We would not damage or violate these places, so why do so many of us (often unintentionally) violate the planet we are lucky enough to visit for a limited time.

And then those who claim to have had visions, or insights from Gods, or angels, or even 'see' ghosts or whatever. Generally, they are treated as of unsound mind, many have been locked up in institutions or just simply ridiculed. Often even those who might listen or believe will keep their thoughts private for fear of the masses.

Which is sad, when just maybe they might be genuine...

We ALL breathe the same air, all people, all creeds, colours, religions, types of organism; now, then and forever to come. We are all connected. We are all one...

We need to be able to let go of the old to be able to receive the new. No one's coming to save us, not now, not ever. And even if they tried to, would we let them?

Tolerance and respect, as ever, would go a long way, and might even just help the whole of the human race...

We are God, as much as any other creature or living entity on this planet. God is us, we are God, we are energy, energy is us. God is energy, energy is God. Energy cannot be created or destroyed. God cannot be created or destroyed.

Believe or not, that's up to you. Maybe religion is the study of cycles?

If energy can neither be created or destroyed, then...

Now

I know a place, a favourite place

End place for the human race

Busy life, always close by

Seems to fade far away

All that noise, no reply

Close by, far away. Here I'll stay

Well, for a while anyway.

An avenue, a road of old

Who once walked here, who was bold

Only you to tell, if yew would tell

Yew who stand, silent, defending

As we through time, slowly turn to soil.

End Notes

P.S. 1. It's funny how the book you end up writing is not necessarily the book you had in mind when you started. This is very definitely the case here. It was just intended to be the series of observations and theories that adorn the second half of the book. The whole first section, the trunk, was just a chapter that I found interesting and maybe had some merit. In fact for a long time, it was so scary that I had decided to leave it out and just include everything else.

It wasn't until I sat down with all my plans at Little Mistletoe that I realised it had to be included and I actually planned out the way it would be. It has changed several times since then, as I read and re read several books I had bought or already had.

It is in no way finished, in fact what I have written is surely no more than the smallest ripple in what must be the vastest and deepest ocean. I haven't even got to circadian rhythms for example. The temptation to abandon the release of the book as it now stands is huge and delve further is intoxicating, but for now I have neither the time nor finances to pursue that dream. I fervently intend to make it a reality. A plan I have in mind.

I will have that plan on paper before you read this. If anyone fancies sponsoring such a project...

P.S. 2. I imagine this book will not stand up to scientific scrutiny. I also have not specifically referenced the books I have on my bookshelves, although I list every book that might have influenced the content. It has largely been written free hand.

P.S. 3. There's a book I read once the main body of the text was finished that changed everything. Whilst everything I wrote here I stand by, there is a further question of conscious thought to answer. Maybe that's 'simple life strategies 3' or maybe not...

P.S. 4. If you fancy joining me on a '5 senses experience' or would like to book me as a speaker for your event please go to www.simplelifecircle.co.uk

The books I have on my shelf.

Esther and Gerry Hicks Ask and It is Given   2004
                                                                  Hay House

Joanna Van Der Hoeven The Awen Alone   2014
                                                                  Moon Books

Shawn Achor   The Happiness Advantage   2010
                                                                  Virgin

Paramhansa Yoganada Autobiography of a Yogi   1946

                                                                  Crystal Clarity

Kristene Marie Corr   Chakras   2016
                                                                  Amazon

Master Choi Kok Sui   The Chakras and their Functions`   2009

                                          IIS publishing Foundation

The Three Initiates   The Kyballion
                                                                  Amazon

Vishvapani Blomfield   Gautama Buddha   2011
                                                                  Quercus

Helwa. A   Secrets of Divine Love   2020
                                                                  Naulit

Lama Yeshe Losal RinpocheFrom a Mountain in Tibet   2020
                                                                  Penguin

Peter Beresford Ellis   Celtic Myths and Legends   1999
                                                                  Robinson

Richard Barber	Myths and Legends of the British Isle	1999
		Boydell & Brewer
Lewis Spence	North American Indians Myths and Legends	
		1994 Senate
John G Neihardt	Black Elk Speaks	1932
		Bison
Shaman Durek	Spirit hacking	2019
		Yellow Kite
Glennie Kindred	Sacred Earth Celebrations	2014
		Permanent
Chris Luttichau	Calling Us Home	2017
		Head of Zeus
Malidoma Patrice	Some Of Water and the Spirit	1994
		Tarcher Putnam
Mudrooroo	Aboriginal Mythology	1994
		Aquarian
Bill Neidjie	Story About Feeling	1989
		Magabala
Thayer Nathanson	Interview with an Angel	1997
		Dell
Malcolm Gladwell	Blink	2003
		Penguin
Johann Hari	Lost Connections	2018
		Bloomsbury
Carol S Dweck	Mindset	2006
		Robinson

Maxwell Maltz	The new Psycho-Cybernetics	2001
		Penguin
Steve Peters	The Chimp Paradox	2012
		Ebury
Williams Pennman	Mindfulness	2011
		Piatkus
Andy Beer	Every Day Nature	2020
		National Trust
Wayne Dyer	Change You Thoughts, Change Your Life	2007
		Hay House

ABOUT THE AUTHOR

Simon lives quietly in deepest darkest East Kent with his wife and son, and canine companions Scruffy and Bruno.

Under the Simple life banner he designs 'wildlife friendy' gardens and leads outdoor experiences drawing on his love of the natural world we live in as the best resource for everything he does to help those who will listen.

Along with his son Ross he also presents the Simple Life Circle, a celebration of all things 'outdoors'.

Printed in Great Britain
by Amazon